That Reminds Me . . .

That Reminds Me...

CANADA'S AUTHORS RELIVE
THEIR MOST EMBARRASSING MOMENTS

MARTA KURC

Stoddart

First published in 1990 by
Stoddart Publishing Co. Limited
34 Lesmill Road
Toronto, Canada
M3B 2T6

CANADIAN CATALOGUING IN PUBLICATION DATA

Main entry under title:

That reminds me-- : Canada's authors relive their
    most embarrassing moments

ISBN 0-7737-2418-4

1. Authors, Canadian (English) - Anecdotes.*
2. Authors, Canadian (English) - Humor.*
3. Canadian wit and humor (English).*
I. Kurc, Marta.

PS8081.T53 1990   C818'.5402   C90-094498-6
PR9186.2.T53 1990

Typesetting: Tony Gordon Ltd.
Printed and bound in Canada

To my mother, my friend

CONTENTS

FOREWORD

ALMOST EVERYONE WILL IDENTIFY with more than one of the embarrassing moments in this wide-ranging and often hilarious collection. W. O. Mitchell is not the only one who has had the dread experience of a balky tap in the washroom; many will identify with D. M. Clark when, as a young man, he tried to buy a condom. I found particular delight in Knowlton Nash's account of a TV control room gone mad; Margaret Atwood on a very different experience in the same category; Eric Wright on mistaken identity; Helen English on ordering food in Mexico. I could go on and name many more delights. It is indeed a rich and varied fare.

What of the editor herself? Marta Kurc, as many of you know, died while this book of hers was being readied for publication. Fortunately, she lived long enough to control its final contents. Marta, with whom I worked for many years, was perhaps the leading authority on author embarrassment in Canada as public relations adviser, coach, shepherd, confidante, chauffeur, buffer and wet nurse to a lengthy list of important Canadian authors. Along the way she experienced — and caused — more than her fair share of embarrassment.

To understand that, you must understand the nature of book promotion. All too often, interviewers — whether on TV, radio or simply for the press — do not read the author's book. Authors were offended by this and blamed Marta.

Some authors even had the nerve to complain about Marta's car. She would always maintain that her stretch limo had broken down and that her little car was an emergency substitute.

Her embarrassments didn't stop there. It wasn't easy for her when she turned up with an author to find out that the schedule had been changed, or when she had to call the producer of a live TV show to say that the author had not arrived; his flight had been postponed.

The truth is, she would put up with almost any imposition from authors and media alike — all for the good of the author. I can think of no one who contributed more to book promotion in Canada than Marta Kurc. Marta was dedicated, a saint, and made a major contribution to authors, the media, booksellers and, ultimately, the public. This book is a most appropriate legacy to her. Read and enjoy.

Jack McClelland

ACKNOWLEDGEMENTS

ONE NICE THING, probably the only nice thing, about not being an author was that I didn't have to submit my own embarrassment experience for this book. Naturally, when I sent out my call for authors' most embarrassing moments, I didn't expect anyone to respond with the really painful, never-to-be-discussed memory, the type that wakes you up at 5:00 a.m. with an "Oh, my God" feeling, nor did they. However, everyone included in the book has been remarkably frank about appearing at a disadvantage and for this I wish to thank them from the bottom of my heart.

The idea for *That Reminds Me . . .* came quite by chance. While I was working at McClelland and Stewart, I was talking on the telephone to author Jo Anne Williams Bennett and mentioned one of my embarrassments. Jo Anne insisted she could top it but said she couldn't relate it by phone — she promised to tell me on her next visit to Toronto "over a stiff drink." She kept her promise and it really was a good story, but out of friendship we agreed not to use it. However, you must get Jo Anne to tell it to you some day.

Special thanks go to: Jo Anne for the idea; Jack Mc-Clelland for his good advice and support throughout; Lily Poritz Miller for using her special magic in capturing many of the contributors; Ted Phillips for submitting the very first piece; Charlotte Vale Allen for her support even before a publisher had been secured; Garry Marchant for his wonderful encouragement and sound advice.

My thanks to *all* the contributors for sharing their experiences so freely.

Marta Kurc

That
Reminds
Me...

MY NEW YORKER STORIES

MANY WRITERS CONSIDER it prestigious to appear in *The New Yorker* magazine, so when I sold the first stories I ever submitted, I felt a certain pride and an increase in self-confidence. I found myself casually mentioning my "*New Yorker* stories" on every possible occasion.

A good one presented itself at a party one evening twenty-odd years ago, after the opening-night performance of *Double Image*, written by Roger MacDougall and myself. The party was hosted by Sir Laurence Olivier and Vivien Leigh, the producers of the play.

Roger and I beamed as we sipped our drinks, listening to the First Nighters assuring us and themselves that we had a "hit."

A bachelor at the time, I cased the Savoy Hotel hall until my eyes fell on a spectacular-looking redhead. I am partial to women with red hair. I am partial to women with any hair colour, but particularly to red. I could feel my nostrils flaring and my virility rising. She was in the midst of a group of women surrounding Sir Laurence (Larry, to his friends), listening wide-eyed to every syllable he uttered.

As one of the playwrights responsible for this successful evening, I resented all the attention being paid to him. Yes, I know. It was *Olivier*. But the guy wasn't even in the play! The evening belonged to Roger and me!

My red-haired lady was staring at him with such adoration, I began to hate him. Outranked and outflanked, I turned my attention to a beautiful brunette with a striking resemblance to Vivien Leigh. I had been too shy during rehearsals to make approaches to Miss Leigh, but now I found myself wine-couraged enough to make a move on her lovely duplicate.

For reasons I no longer can recall, I began explaining General De Gaulle's economic policies. Something to do with adding or removing two decimal points and thereby increasing the value of the franc. I had the brunette's full attention.

I then overheard Sir Laurence (or Larry, if you will) mentioning a favourable theatrical review that had recently appeared in *The New Yorker*, and the redhead exclaiming, "*The New Yorker*! Oh, I love their short stories!"

Switching swiftly from French finance to English literature, I manoeuvred the brunette into a position near the redhead. Did my dark-haired friend happen to read *The New Yorker*? Thankfully, she did, so I was able to casually mention my stories.

Quickly the redhead turned from Sir Laurence. "Did I hear you say you'd had stories published in *The New Yorker*?" she asked, smiling deliciously.

The brunette forgotten, I nodded with a modest smile. I knew the redhead was mine. One knows these things. Then, from a few feet away, I heard a man's voice. "How many stories have you published in *The New Yorker*?"

I ignored the question.

"More than ten?" the voice insisted.

Conversation ceased. Everyone, including Vivien Leigh,

turned to that voice. Its owner was over six feet tall, mustached, wearing a tweed jacket and grey flannel slacks, every inch the country squire, a perfect representative of a lazy, stupid land-owning class with still too much power in England.

The only trouble with this appraisal was that his accent was pure New Yorkese.

"Less than ten?" he persisted.

I realized that I had to do something, so I nodded.

"Less than eight?" — with a slight rise of his bushy eyebrows.

All attention was now focussed on the two of us. I nodded again.

"Less than six?"

A hush dropped on the room. (Was Miss Leigh still looking at me?) I nodded again.

"Less than four?"

Who was this son-of-a-bitch? Why was he doing this to me?

"Less than three?"

My mouth went dry.

"Less than two?"

"No!" I shouted. "Not *less* than two! I've had two stories published in *The New Yorker*! How many have *you* published there?"

I flung the question like a gauntlet, feeling a momentary twinge of pity. The others smiled, awaiting his response, sharing my pleasure at his discomfort.

"A few hundred," came the reply. "I write under the name of S. J. Perelman."

Everyone laughed. So did I. The redhead wafted towards him, the brunette returned to Sir Laurence, and I departed soon afterwards, humbled — hating myself, Sir Laurence, women, but particularly S. J. Perelman.

Years later I had the opportunity to confront my tormen-

3

tor at the apartment of a mutual friend in New York.

"Why did you do that to me in London?"

"Sorry about that," he said, "but I saw her first."

A BEDTIME STORY

SOME TIME AGO, in another country, I met a charming and most delightful man. At the end of our first meeting, he invited me out to dinner a few nights hence, and I accepted eagerly. In what seemed to be true romantic fashion, this man expressed great interest in seeing me again, and I looked forward to what I was sure would be the start of something very nice.

To qualify: something nice, in this case, translates into an ongoing, open-weave sort of affair necessitated by the fact that the gentleman in question and I lived in two different countries separated by a substantial ocean. However, being of an optimistic nature and believing that all things are possible, I prepared for our second meeting with that heightened sense of anticipation that comes when one has met someone around whom it is all too easy to project any number of delectable scenarios. And since my primary talent is one of creating book-length tales from the merest thread of an idea, I had no difficulty envisioning future, and regular, jaunts back and forth across the ocean to facilitate the ongoing affair I was so readily able to imagine.

Well, the dinner was very pleasant. The man was very pleasant. After dinner, we took a stroll through a light evening mist and by the return leg of our leisurely walk, my waist was nicely encircled by the gentleman's arm — an encouraging sign that things were proceeding well. Contact had been made.

Back at my hotel we said good night. I was the recipient of a pair of continental kisses and the promise that we would dine again together the following week.

In the course of the next year, there were quite a number of lunches and dinners each time I had occasion to be in the country. And a certain pattern was established. I would let him know when I would be arriving. He would send flowers to my hotel. I'd telephone upon arrival, and we'd make a date. We'd meet and he would express genuine-seeming delight at seeing me again. We'd talk and eat, and in the course of the time spent together he'd make any number of half gestures — his hand would move to touch my hand or arm, as if of its own accord. Then awareness, or inhibition, or something, would click in and the gesture would be aborted. Periodically, feeling sympathetic, I would make good on the gestures he appeared unable — too shy, too fearful, too something — to complete.

And so a fair amount of hand-holding and gentle teasing got done. There were a number of embraces, and relatively chaste little kisses were given and received. All in all, not quite the scenario I'd originally envisioned. And yet there was no indication of a lack of willingness but rather, I thought, an inability on his part to get to the next logical step in the proceedings.

And so, being a woman of a certain age and experience, I decided that I would have to be the one to make the definitive move. I spent some time considering the pros and cons, concluded I didn't mind taking a calculated risk and went about setting up the circumstances that would make it possible for this very nice, very charming man to make good on those many, many half gestures.

It had been agreed that we would dine together on the night before I was due to return home. In the course of the conversation when we made the date, I said (profoundly and most meaningfully, I thought), "Obviously, you want this decision made for you." To which he replied positively. Given this go-ahead, I forged on, saying, "You know how you always ring me from the lobby to say you're here? Well, when you arrive on Tuesday evening, come directly up to my room." Very overt. But just to make sure there was no doubt of my meaning, I made mention of the fact that instead of the usual twin-bedded room, the hotel had given me one with a double bed. It didn't seem possible anyone could misinterpret the meaning of this highly pointed remark. The date set, the terms — as I'd outlined them — agreed to, I went about my business, planning with enthusiasm the details of the seduction.

Since it was summer, I experimented with various light levels — drawing the curtains, judiciously turning lights on and off — until I had what I felt was an appropriately ambient glow. I had some good moody music on cassette, and the machine with which to play it. I had some nifty lingerie and a wonderfully frothy robe. I had champagne. I was having a hell of a good time setting this particular stage. Theatre on a small scale, dramatic and intriguing. Of course, I'd never done anything quite like this before. But what the hell! Just because in the past the men I'd known had always been the ones to initiate romantic involvements didn't mean one couldn't be flexible. After all, this was the eighties; women were emancipated, free agents. So why not play this out? The added fillip was the fact that, with morning, I'd be leaving, flying off home. So if the gentleman succumbed to the low light, the music, the champagne and the nifty lingerie, it would be up to him to make the next move that would effect a continuation of the affair.

On the afternoon of the day we were to have our final rendezvous of this visit, I raced about town to various meetings, then flew back to my hotel to get everything ready for the evening.

Since I'd rehearsed several times the various preliminary steps, I was bathed and ready, scented and bedecked in the nifty lingerie, well in advance of the gentleman's scheduled arrival. I sat down with a cigarette to watch the news on TV, somewhat distractedly considering the several possible outcomes this evening might have. There was the distinct possibility that "something very nice" was about to begin in earnest. There was also the possibility that, as had happened in the past, I'd gone flying ahead to involve myself wholeheartedly in something that simply didn't exist. But that hardly seemed reasonable in view of our fairly explicit telephone conversation some days earlier.

The telephone rang precisely on the dot of seven, causing me to leap out of the chair like an electrified marionette. I answered. I invited the gentleman to come upstairs. Clearly, he'd elected to follow his previous pattern of ringing from the lobby, despite my advance invitation to come to the room.

With a check of the lighting, the music at just the right volume and my frothy robe floating around me, I went to the door to await his knock. Scrupulously, I avoided my reflection in the hall mirror.

A knock at the door. Keeping carefully out of sight, I opened the door and the gentleman entered. I closed the door with a soft laugh, and presented myself. In the dim light, my friend came as close to a case of cardiac arrest as I've ever witnessed. He turned quite grey, broke out into a sweat, looked around as if for an exit and began burbling nonsense.

The moment of truth. Not only was he utterly unprepared for a full frontal assault on his sensibilities, but he'd completely misunderstood every last remark I'd made in the course of our recent telephone conversation. What to do? There I stood, a middle-aged, somewhat raddled pixie in nifty lingerie and yards of froth, debating whether to go completely insane with self-inflicted embarrassment or to treat the whole thing matter-of-factly and rescue both of us.

I had no choice, really, but to rescue us both. So I invited the fellow to sit down while I drew the curtain a bit to let in some light. Then I lit another cigarette and said I'd just have a smoke before I got dressed and we went out, as planned, for our dinner.

Visibly defensive and still apprehensive, he sat in one chair while I sat in the other with my yards of froth pulled protectively around me, and we discussed business for the seven or eight minutes it took me to smoke the cigarette. Then I whipped into the bathroom with an armload of clothes and proceeded to try to dress, all the while suppressing a sudden, quite overwhelming, desire to laugh myself silly. Saving face, however, being the order of the day, I kept the laughter down, managed to dress myself, then hurried to drag the poor man out into the safety of the hallway.

Over dinner my friend proceeded rapidly and desperately to down one large goblet of wine after another until I asked him with a chuckle if he intended to get seriously drunk simply because I'd found him sufficiently appealing to offer myself to him like a rather bizarre canapé. At this juncture, eased by the wine and by the fact that I was obviously not going to make any sort of a fuss but instead treat the whole matter lightly, he began to relax and then to explain that he preferred to be the one to make decisions of this sort, to be the one to choose the where and when and so forth in an affair. All very interesting, I thought, but too late. While he rambled on about his preferences and his need to be the one in control of certain situations, I sat and listened, gladder than hell that I was leaving first thing in the morning. It appeared I didn't, after all, really want to become involved with someone who not only couldn't make a decision even though he preferred to be the one to make them, but someone who lacked the ability to respond to impulse. A nice man, but not the guy in all those little scenarios.

We had a pleasant dinner. We walked back to my hotel. We exchanged those irritating continental kisses. He went off home. I flew home the next morning.

We're still friends. Neither of us mentions my small theatrical venture. I prefer not to recall it. I've decided it's safer and infinitely less demoralizing to write about the things I imagine rather than attempting to bring them to life. And who knows? Maybe these things work for other people. Maybe it was the wrong nifty lingerie. Or could it have been the frothy robe . . . or the music . . . or was it maybe too dark . . . ?

A FLYING START

IN ADULT LIFE, my most embarrassing moments have come during other people's introductions to my readings. What do you do when the man introducing you proposes to read the audience the entire last chapter of your novel, gets your name wrong or characterizes you as some kind of machine-gun-wielding radical terrorist?

But my first moment of truly public embarrassment occurred when I was fourteen. It was the early days of CBC television, and things were kind of improvised. Many shows were live. There was usually just one camera; there was little editing. Much joy was contributed to the world, in those days, by the howlers, faux pas, bloopers and pratfalls that were sent out, uncensored, over the airwaves.

The woman who lived next door, and for whom I baby-sat, had somehow become the producer of a show called "Pet Corner," a title that is self-explanatory. At that time, in lieu of cats, I had a beautiful, green, intelligent praying mantis called Lenore (after the Poe poem, not after my future sister-in-law), which lived in a large jar, ate insects and drank sugar water out of a spoon. (For those who may accuse me of cruelty to insects, let me point out that this was, a) an old praying mantis, which had b) already laid its egg-mass, and which c) lived a good deal longer in my jar than it would have outside, as it was d) cold out there.) My neighbour thought this would be a good thing to have on "Pet Corner," so I went, praying mantis, spoon and all, and presumably electrified the audience with an account of what female praying mantises would eat if they could get any, namely male praying mantises.

Lenore was such a hit that "Pet Corner" decided to have me back. This time I was to be merely an adjunct. A woman was coming onto the show with a tame flying squirrel; I was to be the person the flying squirrel flew to, a sort of human tree.

All went as scheduled up to the time of the flight. Flying squirrels were explained, this one was produced (close shot), then raised on high, aimed and fired. But flying squirrels are nocturnal, and it was annoyed by the bright television lights. When it landed on me, it immediately went down my front.

At my school we wore uniforms: black stockings, bloomers, white blouses and a short tunic with a belt and a large square neckline. It was this neckline that the squirrel utilized; it then began scrabbling around beneath, and could be seen as a travelling bulge moving around my waistline, above the belt. (Close shot.) But it was looking for something even more secluded. I thought of the bloomers, and swiftly reached down the front of my own neckline. Then I thought better of it, and began to lift the skirt. Then I thought better of that as well. Paralysis. Nervous giggling. At last the owner of the flying squirrel fished the thing out via the back of my jumper.

Luckily the show went on during school hours, so none of my classmates saw it. Not much that has gone on at public readings since then has been able to compete in embarrassment value; not even the times I fell off the podium, had a nosebleed or had to be whacked on the back by James Reaney ("Harder!" I gasped. "Harder!") because I was choking to death. Maybe it's for this reason that I always have trouble spelling "embarrassment." I keep thinking it should have three e's.

WOMAN TALK

IT MUST HAVE BEEN early fall, but memory puts it in the spring. April probably. One of those overcast, blustery, not-quite-cold April days when the landscape is drained of colour and nothing has a shadow.

Friends had come over for the afternoon. I was sitting inside with Jackie in the cabin living room. A wood fire crackled in the stove. We sat there in the over-warm room discussing the indignities of motherhood. It was several lifetimes back — almost twenty years ago. I had only just had my first child and Jackie was heavy with hers. It was likely she still believed in childbirth without pain and I didn't want to be the one to disillusion her. So we didn't talk much about labour and delivery. Instead, we chatted about waking and sleeping, and not sleeping. About diapers, baby clothes and breastfeeding, topics on which I was now an expert.

We made tea. We inveighed against the invasive practices of doctors, the discomforts of prenatal exams, the fist rammed up our bottoms, the cold, rubber-gloved hands wallowing about inside us, prodding and poking into places

14

we never knew we had to protect. And why, we wondered, must we be shaved in order to give birth? Why the mandatory enemas? The women's movement was still only a whisper. We didn't understand how much hatred had been institutionalized.

Our husbands were outside working on something. Maybe it was the porch roof. Whatever it was, they were very busy with it. This seems to be something most men get into when their wives become pregnant. They start building on to the house, or they buy a new house, or they change their jobs. Or they do all three. Some sort of male nesting instinct. But the last thing you want when you're eight months gone is packing cases or plaster board all over the house.

They were standing out there in the wind discussing the best way to go about whatever it was they were doing. Ken rubbed his chin thoughtfully and Dave pointed with the hammer. They agreed, they disagreed, they considered, they compromised. They examined various pieces of wood. They made their voices sound deep and knowledgeable. They were outside playing at their male role and we were inside playing at ours.

I put a piece of maple in the stove. We had moved on from motherhood to chronicle other embarrassments of being female. The strained reactions of our fathers to our first periods. Our mortification when our mothers refused any longer to buy Kotex for us. How unpleasant, almost frightening we had found our first "internal" examinations, those inspections done by strange doctors in cities new to us: the shock of the steel-cold speculum, the unanticipated stretching as the device was jacked apart — like being pried open by a mammoth boot-tree. All for the sake of medical convenience. Once, a speculum like that got stuck inside me. The doctor couldn't remove it. He tugged, he sweated, he apologized in a small voice. It was a rare, unforgettable moment of panic for both patient and physician.

We were speaking very softly because it was time for the baby to wake from his nap. I wanted him to sleep on a little longer. I wanted to squeeze in as much time as possible with a fellow adult before I was once more monopolized by a possessive infant.

Outside a stranger had arrived. Some wandering young man with a beard and red kerchief, though his hair was un-fashionably short. I had never seen him before. Perhaps he was visiting one of the local communes. Perhaps he was a hitchhiker. He was talking with Ken and Dave about what to do with the porch.

Knowing he was there, we dropped our voices further. We were onto the juicy stuff now. Disease: yeasts, fungi, monilia, candida, thrush. Suppositories and douches. The works. Did you get it from antibiotics? From a boyfriend? What was your doctor like? Was a woman gynecologist better than a man?

We started giggling because we had never talked about these things with each other and there was a release in getting them out in the open. It was a kind of exorcism.

"The worst thing," I said to Jackie, leaning close to keep my voice as low as possible. "The absolutely most embarrassing thing that ever happened to me . . ."

I broke off, smirking.

She nodded, what?

"The worst thing was when I went to the doctor . . ."

She chuckled.

" . . . and he told me . . ."

We were both snickering now, anticipating the punch line.

" . . . he told me . . ." I unfettered my voice, raising it up. I let the words ride forth on a wave of laughter.

" . . . he said I had *warts on my cunt!*"

I trumpeted out those words just as the strange young man in the kerchief walked into the living room.

Silence hit us like a slap.

The young man walked to the other side of the room. He mumbled a formless "hello" as he passed. He stood a few seconds by the stove, making a point of not looking at us. Then he left.

Jackie began to wriggle about. She lay back in her chair, put her hands on her large belly and rolled from side to side with glee.

"He must have heard me," I said to her, dismayed.

She nodded, oh yes.

"But he didn't say anything."

"What could he say?" wondered Jackie between snorts and hiccups.

She was right, of course. You have to be quite self-possessed to recover from that kind of entrance. And you probably need to be older than the strange young man in the kerchief.

I began to laugh along with Jackie. We looked through the curtains for the strange young man, but he was nowhere about. So we let go, we went right out of control. We sobbed with mirth. We shrieked and wept and our bodies ached with it. We stopped every so often, but then one of us would start up again in those soft, helpless, coughing spasms, and the other would be reinfected.

Baby slept through everything.

Our husbands heard our merriment and they looked solemnly through the windows. They tapped on the panes and asked what was wrong. We couldn't tell them yet, so we locked them out of the house and laughed that much harder to see their cross, disapproving expressions.

Ken worried about Jackie. "Are you all right?" he mourned, his face plaintive and long through the glass. Maybe he thought she would go into premature labour. He said over and over, "What's so funny?" and "Why won't you let us inside?"

Dave gave him the old what can you expect with all those hormones? look. Or perhaps he was afraid we were laughing at *him* and didn't want to let on he was worried. Who knows? There was no sign of our visitor. He never came by again.

When we had calmed down at last, we let them back into the house and we told them why we were laughing.

Neither of them thought it was funny.

D. M. CLARK

A Delicate Transaction

IN THE MID-FIFTIES when I was too old for short pants, but still too stupid to be of much use to anyone, even myself, there was an air of innocence that by a decade later had disappeared.

Hormones raged while your imagination went wild, and most times your brain couldn't keep up. A nymphomaniac might enter your bedroom at night because she needed it bad. On your way to school you could be shoved into the bush by a lithesome beauty who couldn't put it off a minute longer. Or hauled into the back seat of some convertible by a young housewife who wasn't getting enough. Somehow a benevolent and merciful God would let this happen to you, knowing you needed it to keep living.

In case any of these wonderful things should come about, you needed to carry a condom in your wallet. It was a sure sign that you had "arrived." No more nightly self-abuse, you were ready for the real thing! Of course that was a promise of short duration.

But in our vast and incredible innocence we were never sure that condoms were even legal, for one thing. Condoms were birth control, and you wouldn't need birth control if you obeyed the "law" of God and Man, and *didn't do it till you were married!* So right away just thinking about it you were in trouble.

Lifting *Zane Grey* magazine was one thing, but suppose some night you were stopped by the law and asked to identify yourself. There would be that telltale little circle in that small pocket of your wallet meant for postage stamps.

"What's this then, son?"

"What, sir?"

"This?"

"A 'thing.'"

"Do you know fornicators use these, son?"

"No, sir."

"Are you a fornicator, son?"

"No, sir."

"Why do you have this in your wallet then?"

"I don't know, sir."

"Aren't the girls in this town safe from you, son?"

"Yes, sir, they are."

"Not with this thing in your wallet."

"I think somebody put it in there, sir, when I wasn't looking. I didn't know about it . . . being illegal?"

You could end up in Condom Court, where they handled hard-core cases like you.

The town drugstore had female clerks. Mrs. Shirley Stavik was one. She was a Mrs., but she was probably less than twenty-five. Her lips were heavy and red and luscious, and she wore bows in her hair. She'd been a Cherry Carnival Queen a few years earlier. We were all smitten.

She was so pure, you could never imagine Mrs. Shirley Stavik "wanting it bad." We bought hot-rod and body-building magazines from her, but you could never go up and ask her for " . . . you knows." But they were there under the counter, we'd heard, and if someone was insensitive enough to ask Mrs. Shirley Stavik for "things," she'd likely reach for them with tongs or at least a rubber glove.

Another thing: did they come in six or a dozen at a time, or could you buy them singly? Was it better to ask for "safes" or "frenchies" instead of condoms? There had to be different kinds, too. But what were their names? Who could you ask?

"Dad, I'm thinking of buying condoms. What kind would you suggest?"

You'd be piling cordwood for the next seventeen years.

Those who already carried them in their wallets kept the secrets of acquisition to themselves. You were on your own.

We had this guy, Steve Andrews. He started shaving in grade three. He wore battered motorcycle boots even during phys ed. When he played soccer, he played alone.

"Steve, you got any condoms in your wallet?"

"Who wants to know?"

"Just asking."

"Where'd you get 'em, Steve?"

"Up your arse!"

We speculated Steve used the condoms on his father's dairy cows.

Then word came from somewhere that condoms could be gotten in the pool hall. Who'd have thought that? But where better to get contraband than from a dim, smoke-filled dive like the pool hall.

Inside, around the perimeter you never knew exactly what was happening. Old guys with three teeth left sat on scarred wooden benches, drinking from brown paper bags. All of them smoked pipes or munched the ends of dead, two-day-old cigars. Some chewed stuff that leaked brown sauce from the corner of their lips.

The shifty-eyed, temporarily or chronically unemployed and ne'er-do-wells chalked their cues, cursed and talked about miraculous shots, booze and loose women. They wore big belt buckles and T-shirts with Export A's or Players stuffed into the sleeves. There was small-time gambling.

In front you could buy tobacco, pipes, lighters, belt buckles, baseball caps, chocolate bars, gum, pop, pocket knives, souvenir spoons and ballpoint pens. There was more.

There was a glass-less window looking into the rear, and most of the time Ben Novicky, who ran the place, leaned on this window talking to his cronies in the back.

"They're under the counter," I was told. "He don't keep 'em where you can see 'em, for Chrissakes!" Fifty cents for a package of three.

I had a good friend, Bert. He needed "frenchies" for his hormones and wallet as badly as I did. We flipped a coin and I lost. Then spent the better part of a morning like guys casing the joint, trying to screw up my courage. After a while Ben began giving us the eye.

"Ain'tcha playin' pool today?"

"Nope."

"You boys be ready to scat outa here, the cops show up."

"Yeah."

He grunted and leaned on the window looking into the rear. He shouted something to someone.

"Huh, Ben?" I said. It was now or never.

"Yeah?" he asked over his shoulder.

"Ben, I . . . uh . . . need somethin' here."

"Yeah?" He turned from the window and came over to the counter. "What?" he said.

"I . . . uh . . . need some . . ." I waved my hand as though he could read that gesture as well as my mind.

He aped the gesture. "An' what the hell is that supposed to mean?"

"Uh, I need some . . . 'safes.' 'Frenchies.' Sort of."

He got this look on his face that made me sorry I'd ever asked. I figured I'd rather be shot and pissed on than be where I was right then.

"Three for fifty cents," he said.

"Yeah, I know." Like I'd been doing this for years.

He bent over beneath the counter. Then a second later peered at me with his chin resting on the edge. "What size?" he asked. "Men's or boys'?"

"Men's size," I said.

At that precise moment a God I wasn't sure I even believed in stilled the universe so that everyone in that pool hall would hear this exchange. The pop machine stopped gurgling, the ubiquitous radio conked out. Not a soul shooting pool in the back made a sound or a move. No balls clacked. The lights over the pool tables ceased humming. Out on the street no car honked a horn.

I sent up a silent prayer, promising to dedicate what was left of my life to God's Works, if He'd just get me through this.

But a second later the house came down. Ben whooped and hollered. Old guys who hadn't laughed at anything since their wives died gagged on their juices. Pool players doubled. Some slapped their thighs, others banged their cues on the floor. Some did both. Fat guys had strokes. Smokers coughed themselves to death. Grown men wept with laughter. In the very back by the exit doors, two guys I knew from high school yelled and called my name. I was now famous. I'd have to leave town, but they'd never forget anyway.

Even my erstwhile friend Bert, who was no wiser than I about the purchase of condoms, figured he'd better get in on it before he looked stupid as I did. Idiocy by association.

Ben mopped his eyes and regained his sanity. He slapped the little packet of condoms on the counter. I took them, thinking that before I ever came in here again, Ben would be dead and his offspring all eating prunes in the old folks' home.

Later I relented and gave one of the condoms to Bert for

his silence. I sold the second to another guy and carried the third in my wallet, though there was little pride in the memory of its purchase.

Then one day in English class I kind of "accidentally" let it slip out and roll down the aisle past a row of giggling girls. Impressive, no? At which time Steve Andrews put his size twelve motorcycle boot on it and ground it into the tiles.

"I thunk it was some kinda insect crawlin' t'wards me," he said.

MATT COHEN

WHERE IS MY BOOK?

RECENTLY I RECEIVED a letter addressed to:

Matt Cohen, B.A., M.A., D.A.

Although the province of Ontario wasted a certain sum of money on my education (curiously, one is never informed of the exact amount, but that is a different subject), I hadn't been aware things had gone so well. To clarify the situation, I rushed to my neighbourhood bookstore and thumbed through the Hurtig Encyclopedia to find my own entry. As my mother had assured me, my name was there. I discovered that I had been born in Montreal (a fact my parents concealed from me, but they probably had their reasons), but there was no mention of my D.A.

Being already in the bookstore, it seemed an excellent opportunity to do some private stockchecking. As always, I discovered my own books were missing. I rushed back home, telephoned my editor, and in a high falsetto voice said that I was a doctoral student from Yugoslavia, in Toronto on a scholarship from the Canadian Department of

External Affairs, and that the books of the only worthwhile living Canadian writer seemed to be unavailable. Were they being reprinted? I inquired.

My editor was, of course, dumbfounded. Only two weeks ago, she said, a publisher from Iceland had telephoned to say that while browsing for great novels in a Bloor Street bookstore he had been amazed to discover that the books of the only etc. were unavailable. She then went on to say that although Mr. Cohen was undeniably a genius, especially in those earlier works which — since they had been published while she was still in public school — she had unfortunately not had time to read, he, on the other hand, had a bit of a reputation as a D.A.

"D.A.? My dear me, we do not have that expression in our Yugoslavian-English lexicon. Is it peculiar to Canada?" I squeaked.

"I don't know," my editor said. "But I can tell you what it means. D.A. means Difficult Author. On the one to ten scale, we rank him a nine."

"Nine?" I said in my high little voice.

"Nine out of ten. To be a ten you have to take your clothes off in public."

"Oh my dear. I don't think Mr. Cohen would do that. I understand his father worked down the hall from an underwear magnate. Good-bye."

As I put down the receiver, I suddenly remembered a terrible incident. While on a book tour, shortly after landing in my sixth city in as many days, I was being driven to the hotel by the publicity person in charge of such things when I asked how she liked my book.

"Not your best," she said. "My favourite is still *The Dispossessed*."

As we got closer to the hotel, I asked if my new mediocrity had preceded me to town. I was hoping she would say, at least, that it was selling well, despite etc.

"No problem," she said. "We have lots of stock to last until Christmas."

"It must be difficult," I said, "having a basement of books."

"We don't have a basement," she said. Then she nodded towards the back of her car. In the glow of a stoplight, I could see there were several cartons of books. The carton marked with my own title was filled with hockey equipment.

When we got to the hotel, my admirer asked if she could make a phone call from my room to verify one of the items on my schedule. In my room, while the telephone was being used, I opened my suitcase and tried to decide whether or not to hang up my jeans.

"Can I borrow your bathroom?"

"Of course."

A few moments later I could hear loud sobbing through the door. Time passed. Until this moment my most embarrassing moment as an author had been the occasion on which, after giving a reading in a northern Ontario library to an audience of three deaf-mutes, I had unthinkingly concluded, "Are there any questions?"

"Is there anything wrong?" I wanted to ask through the bathroom door. On the other hand, things were obviously not going too well.

As the sounds intensified, I reviewed my own behaviour on the trip from the airport. I must be, I realized, one of dozens of writers who had come to town expecting fame, publicity, interviews on exercise shows. How could I have been so tactless as to ask about the fate of my own worthless book when in fact it was only one of hundreds currently oversaturating the market? And who had the unsavory job of trying to cram one more drop into the already dripping sponge? The poor overworked promotion person who even now was only beginning to gain control.

You must hate me, I wanted to call through the door. I don't blame you. I hate myself.

In the long silence that followed this unspoken declaration, I had a vision of our vast country, and in this vision bookstores were spread coast to coast. In each of those bookstores the piles of my books were gathered up and put into cartons to be sent back to the publisher. I was relieved, in this vision, to know that never again would I embarrass myself or my fellow human beings by attempting to sell a book.

I was still basking in the glory of this vision when the bathroom door opened. The face of my friend — because through our shared ordeal she had become my friend — was still stained with tears.

"I'll see you tomorrow," she said. "Be in the lobby at eight o'clock."

AND THAT'S THE WAY IT WAS

IT WASN'T EMBARRASSING at the time; the embarrassment grew as the years passed. Now I can hardly bear to think about it. Could I have ever been that naive?

As a teenage copy boy at the Montreal *Gazette* in the 1950s, I thought that I was pretty sophisticated. In imitation of the reporters on the newspaper, I smoked a lot, drank too much and kept my tie unknotted and the collar of my raincoat turned up (the only affectation that still sticks). I accepted uncritically the self-image that older journalists projected. The city editor of *The Gazette* was a particular hero.

Harry — he's dead now but I'll use a pseudonym anyway — was a concert pianist *manqué*. Come to think of it, the newsroom was filled with might-have-beens: the sportswriter who might have been a great lawyer, the religious editor who might have been a great preacher, and all of us who might have been great novelists. Harry might have been a great pianist — he had a narrow intellectual face, long tapering hands and a fiery temperament — but something had gotten in the way. It was probably alcohol but by the time I knew Harry, booze had clearly become the result and chief consolation of this great tragedy rather than its cause.

I don't want to make Harry sound like a broken-down alcoholic because he wasn't. Although he seemed much older to me then, he probably was only in his forties. He was a skilful editor of remarkable sensitivity, for that era, whose personal difficulties were compounded by this situation in which he found himself at *The Gazette*. Everyone knew that Harry was competing with the news editor for the managing editor's job and that he was doomed to lose. The news editor drank even more than Harry, wore cowboy boots and was as hard as nails. It was evident that he was going to march all over Harry on his way to the top. (In the end, neither got the job.)

When Harry was drinking, he was much more sociable than the news editor ever was. I had even helped older journalists (look, everybody, I'm one of *them*) to carry him home from office parties. He lived in a small apartment in lower Westmount that wouldn't satisfy a cub reporter in the 1990s, let alone a city editor, but at that time it seemed the height of urban sophistication. Even in the dim light of dawn, as we tripped over milk bottles on the way into his apartment, I could barely bring myself to look at his wife because I knew Harry's secret.

Late one night, when I was clearing copy from the teletype machines for the last time, Harry had phoned to ask me to bring him a bottle. He was at his mistress's. I delivered the bottle and was given a drink for my trouble (more a friend than a messenger boy, you see, but I don't want to be too cynical; I like to think Harry really did enjoy my company). I don't remember the mistress at all, but her nasty Siamese cat sticks in my memory. Whenever Harry appeared for work with scratches on his hands, I knew where he had been.

The only other people I knew who had mistresses were the artists and writers that I hung around with on Stanley

Street. It was the 1950s, as I've said, and the first Hungarian coffee houses had just opened on Stanley with tables on the sidewalk. It was just like Paris or Greenwich Village, we all thought, even if espresso was the strongest drink available. Barely out of high school, still physically awkward and emerging slowly from a splatter of acne that had been my first experience of the wilful inequity of providence, I was tolerated by the older bohemians and younger beatniks because I wrote stories about them in *The Gazette*. They provided me with my first subjects for bylined feature articles, I provided *The Gazette* with free copy from an unexpected source, and everyone was happy.

Despite my growing sense of self-importance, I was mildly suspicious when Harry asked me one night if I would be free for dinner the following Saturday. The last such invitation, from the news editor with the cowboy boots, had produced several hours of carrying rocks out of his garden by way of hors d'oeuvres before I had received a meagre supper. But this one certainly sounded like the real thing. It was to be black tie, in a penthouse in upper Westmount.

The party, explained Harry, would be a fine occasion for me to meet a friend of his, an investment dealer of some sort. I could chat with this financial wizard and if I thought he was interesting — it was up to me, of course — I might be inclined to write one of my feature stories about him. Harry was always very encouraging about my writing and for him, I would have tried to interview a garden slug. And, said Harry, bring a girl.

That was a problem. I could rent a tux but where could I find a suitable companion? Harry had painted an exalted picture of the splendour of the occasion and I knew that the survivors of high-school romances from my middle-class neighbourhood of Notre-Dame-de-Grace were out of the question. I needed a woman of the world.

My Stanley Street friends came to the rescue. When the

big evening arrived, I drove up Côte-des-Neiges boulevard in my father's car, arrayed in a rented tux and with a borrowed mistress by my side. She had been loaned to me by a sculptor. I no longer remember her name, but I do recall handling her as if she were made of TNT. I think I must have been afraid that any sudden movement on my part would set her off, with terrible repercussions in the sculptor's studio. Torn by fear, chivalry and sexual desire, I was a bundle of nerves when I finally rang the bell of the penthouse and shook hands with the butler.

Well, why not? He was dressed exactly as I was. But after the genuine host appeared, and a few drinks had been consumed, I began to feel that I really belonged in this elevated world. It was the first two-storey penthouse that I had seen outside the movies. In fact, I remember the whole scene — the liveried servants, the sumptuous buffet dinner, the stratospheric patio overlooking the slopes of Mount Royal and lights of downtown Montreal — in grainy black and white. Even the star of the evening, when we were finally closeted in the mahogany-panelled library, looked more like Orson Welles than an investment dealer. He was an enormous man and a perfect interview subject. As I delved for pencil and pad in the pockets of my dinner jacket, I mentally composed opening paragraphs about "the biggest investment dealer in the city."

I wrote something like that the next day, a quiet Sunday afternoon in the newsroom. Harry handled the story himself, marking it up and sending it along to the composing room. Only when the first copies of the paper came up from the pressroom did the managing editor suddenly rush out of his office, paper in hand, to have a hurried conversation with Harry. Then he hurried downstairs to the mailroom.

None of this involved me. I heard later that friends of the so-called investment dealer were already in the mailroom, buying copies of the newspaper with its valuable article as they rolled from the press. (Within a few days, I've no doubt, the copies were adding a nice touch of respectability to his brochures touting real estate in Florida, mining shares in British Columbia or whatever). The press run was immediately stopped and the offending piece yanked from the page before printing resumed.

I don't know what transpired between the managing editor and the city editor after that, but on the surface, everything continued as usual. Harry remained as city editor. The reporters in the Press Gallery in Quebec City continued to receive their annual "stationery allowances" from the government. Suburban councils in Montreal continued to pay the paper's suburban reporter for covering their meetings. Money was routinely paper-clipped to press releases handed to Montreal journalists. Reporters never paid parking tickets. And mysterious stories, usually about various business ventures, continued to appear in the city's newspapers from time to time without any apparent reason.

It was only in the 1960s that politicians and journalists in Montreal started to worry about ethics — the politicians led the way, as I recall — and that I began to feel embarrassed by many of the practices that I had taken for granted. But the worst memory of all is shaking hands with the butler.

SOMETIMES ONE COOK IS TOO MANY

ONE OF THE UNFORTUNATE side effects of writing about Benny Cooperman is the impression that the author, like the character, lives almost exclusively on chopped egg sandwiches, white milk and white bread. I admit that, for my own reasons, Benny, the gumshoe from Grantham, Ontario, does live on a restrictive diet. His eating is habit-ridden, unadventurous and boring. Benny hasn't been around much. Unlike his creator, who has lived in France, Spain, Cyprus and England, Benny is a hometown kid, who buttons up tight before hitting the road from Grantham to Toronto. It sometimes irks me when it is grandly assumed that our tastes are alike.

I would like to take this opportunity to say that I enjoy food. I like eating out, trying new things and even bashing about in the kitchen. Yes, I enjoy cooking. I wouldn't go so far as to say that I'm a gourmet or a chef among my friends, but I take pleasure in pots and pans. I will make a detour in my travels to a good kitchen-supply store and a trip to a first-rate market is always worth the journey in itself. Benny Cooperman would never find paella or zarzuela palatable.

His mother would wonder where he ever heard of garlic soup or cassoulet. What he would do with a *boeuf en daube* is anybody's guess. Unless you called it stew, he'd jump to dessert. Benny would be happier if it all came out of a can, like vegetable soup.

But once it all turned out badly. Once something happened that made me retreat into my shell never to come out again, well never again wearing a chef's bonnet. It happened in Spain during the summer of 1960. At that time I was living in an old house, high in the old Balearic town of Ibiza. I had been cooking for myself over a charcoal stove and the results, using local spices and herbs, were encouraging.

One day, I invited the New York painter and public prankster Alberto Carlo and his house guests for dinner. My place was large enough and the windows in the front room looked down over an ancient balcony on a courtyard below, full of women in black knitting, crocheting, while their men fashioned rope-soled shoes beside the bead curtains of their front doorways. I decided to make something simple, earthy, basic: spaghetti and meatballs with a Bolognese sauce as a main course.

Buying meat in Ibiza was always a difficult affair. Beef hadn't been seen since the last bullfight and that was five years ago. The normal fare in the few butcher shops was mutton or goat, which was cut from a carcass suspended from a hook. If you wanted good cuts, you had to be there early. For latecomers all that was left was the scrag-end of neck. The idea of cutting up the beast except for immediate sale had not penetrated this far at that time. I got the butcher to grind the piece of goat I bought and took it home.

In order to bind my meatballs together, I needed eggs. There were none to be had for love or money anywhere within range of my rented bicycle. Flour, I thought, flour will bind as well as eggs, and I got to work among the earthen-

ware pots over the charcoal. Somehow, the meatballs refused to stay together. They wanted to join the sauce. Well,
more flour was obviously called for.

While I was wrestling with the problem of the dissolving
meatballs, I got a message requesting that I bring the meal
out to Carlo's villa in Las Figueretas, about a ten-minute
ride from the old city gates on my bike. There were apologies and offers of help in making the transfer after I declined
the suggestion that my invitation be postponed until a more
convenient evening. It was the arrival of fresh house guests
that necessitated this late change of plans. I was so involved
with my spaghetti and meatballs, I didn't consider being
miffed at Carlo. I didn't even think about the logistics of getting a hot meal from high in the walled town to Figueretas.
This was still some decades before Meals-on-Wheels.

Somehow I managed to sling all my pots and dishes to
the bicycle and arrived at the villa without incident. I'd been
looking forward to meeting Gunn, the daughter of Victor
Seaström, the Swedish film director who discovered Garbo
and later himself starred in Bergman's *Wild Strawberries*.
Others gathered around the table were Jack Longini, an
American disc jockey, and his girlfriend, Lorca, Rosalyn
Tobias, a New York casting director, a producer named
Harry Kantor, a couple of people from Barcelona and Phillip
Freiberg, a former Las Vegas croupier. The soup was served
by the regular cook without betraying any sign that her nose
was out of joint because Carlo had brought in his Canadian
friend to cook on this special occasion. The soup was just
passable. There was much rubbing of hands and tucking in
of napkins as the sauce and meatballs were passed around.
Then the tasting began. Silence. Silence in several languages. Even to me, the cook, it tasted like glue. I'd put that
down to having been tasting the mixture since early in the
morning when I'd started cooking. More silence, and Carlo,

our host, looked at all of those forks suspended above the bowls of spaghetti. Carlo cleared his throat at last and said, "Howard, you are essentially a writer, are you not?" That broke the ice and the salad was served.

A Light Breakfast

Ignorance of language never deterred me from attempts to communicate with local people the world over. As a journalist and more recently a travel photographer, I have found it expedient to learn at least a few phrases including those of common courtesy. This modicum of the mother tongue of whatever country one happens to be visiting eases one's way and often evokes delight on the part of the local people. While I'm sure to have insulted many, most have good-naturedly forgiven my faux pas and responded graciously.

One caution to enthusiastic would-be linguists in foreign lands: beware the idiom! The whimsical regional connotations of some words and phrases may leave you tongue-tied with embarrassment. No language courses, which by their very nature must generalize, will prepare you for this eventuality. Add to that the complication of the fact that the whole world over, people from one region of a country tend to make disparaging comments about those from the next. We aren't the only ones with "Newfie-type" jokes.

The beauty of Mexico and warm hospitality of its people draws me back time and time again. I've travelled extensively through several regions via different means of transportation, including over fifteen hundred miles by local buses, and have always been treated kindly. I have yet to explore the northern regions bordering the U.S.

While visiting an archaeological dig in the Chicontepec oil fields, my friends and I stayed at a small hotel in the Gulf Coast town of Tuxpan. A problem with our car brought several PEMEX engineers working a nearby oil rig construction site to our rescue. They were mostly Mexican with, in this instance, one Portuguese and one American thrown into the mix.

Since they stayed at our hotel, it was quite natural that we should join them in the dining room on occasion. Breakfast the morning in question was no exception. After the usual round of pleasantries, I settled in with a steaming bowl-sized *café con leche* to study the extensive menu. Normally, I'd just motion to the waiter to bring me whatever my friends, the engineers, were having. However, due to a bout of late night "disco fever" — absolutely the only entertainment in the oil-crazed boom town — my stomach cried out for tenderness. As a food writer travelling the world in search of recipes for my *Globe and Mail* columns, I was generally blessed with a cast-iron stomach. On this occasion, however, no hair of the Chihuahua would soothe it. Poached eggs on toast offered the likeliest balm.

My slightly paunchy waiter, a man with a kindly air and the patience of Job, arrived at the table before I could locate the desired item on the menu. He hovered over me, check form and pen poised, attentive as though I might say something momentous. Something worth engraving for posterity?

I plunged in with my best learned-by-rote Spanish, *"Traigame dos huevos poches, por favor."*

His eyebrows instantly arched up his forehead in such exaggeration I thought they might attach themselves permanently to the Elvis-style dollop of his vaselined pompadour.

There was an embarrassing hush at the table as all eyes turned on me.

What's wrong? I wondered silently, knowing full well the use of this very phrase brought exactly the desired results in any other area of Mexico that I had visited previously.

Before I could interject, he leaned forward like some priest about to hear confession, hands holding pen and pad pressed together in prayerlike attitude, "Are you *sure?*" A stage whisper.

Slightly irritated by the unwanted attention my table companions were now paying my culinary taste, I retorted quickly and confidently, "Of course, I'm sure!"

My self-confidence melted as laughter broke like thunder from all quarters . . . engineers and waiter alike. Not being party to the joke, I could only wait, red-faced, for the frivolity to subside.

Taking pity on my befuddlement, the American engineer explained, sotto voce, that in this area of Mexico people looked down on countrymen in the northern regions who tried to enter the U.S. illegally. Scorning the American descriptive of "wetbacks," they had their own colourful expression. Laughingly, they made reference to the fact that such would-be emigrés, in crossing the shallow, warm waters of the Rio Grande, got a certain portion of their male anatomy wet in the process and thus conferred on them the nickname of "Huevos Poches."

My blissfully ignorant foray into the vagaries of the Mexican vernacular had, for the first time, caused me to lose my appetite. I decided to forgo breakfast.

A Star Is Born

BEFORE I STARTED WRITING, my ambition was to be an actress. I loved performing and had visions of a great career on both the stage and screen. Unfortunately, though I can carry a tune, it was obvious from a fairly early age that it was unlikely I would achieve such stardom in any role that required me to open my mouth in song. Still, I tried, performing in such musicals as *Good News* and *Little Me*, and even auditioning for the part of the eldest daughter in Norman Jewison's movie version of *Fiddler on the Roof*, an audition that went splendidly until I was asked to give my vocal rendition of the song "Matchmaker." I don't think I'll ever forget the stunned silence that accompanied my rendition, nor the looks of unadulterated wonder emanating from the faces of those present at that audition. In case there is any doubt, I did not get the part, though, without question, it would have been a celluloid moment to remember.

I should have had an inkling, I suppose, of the effect my voice could have on mere mortals, since I had been through a somewhat similar experience at university. During my years at the University of Toronto, I appeared in over twenty plays, many of which took place during lunch hour on the delightful stage of the Women's Union Theatre on St. George Street. One such play was a little-produced example of the Theatre of the Absurd, the name of which has totally escaped me. It was a three character play whose plot — if such it can be called — defies description. All I can clearly remember about any of it is that at some point in the production, the action called for me to turn on the radio and announce to the other actors (whose names were Hersh and Nomi) that it was time to listen to my favourite hymn. At this point, the three of us would stand very still and pay rapt attention to the song being played. The sound man, off-stage, was responsible for supplying the appropriate tape. All went well for the first several performances, but on the third day, as I stepped jauntily to the radio and pressed the correct button, instead of the music I expected, I was greeted with the sound of a loud stage whisper from the wings announcing that the tape wasn't working.

I remember the most ominous silence as I stood there, trying to decide what to do. My voice quivering, I announced to one and all that the radio was on the fritz, and so I was going to have to do the job myself. I stepped forward, much to the horrified looks of my co-stars. Hersh told me later that all he could think of was, "Oh, my God, surely she's *not* going to sing!" But sing I did. Occupying centre stage, my shoulders thrust proudly back, my head loftily raised, I belted into that fragile little hymn for all I was worth. The audience grew absolutely still. And then, midway through my performance, I became aware of muffled sounds from somewhere behind me. I turned around — still singing — to see Hersh and Nomi absolutely doubled over with laughter. The audience, bless their confused little hearts, had no idea what was going on. Because the action seemed no less puzzling than anything else in the play up until that point, many thought my singing and the accompanying hysterics of my co-stars were part of the play. Even now, over twenty years later, I can't think of that time without laughing — and without turning a bright red.

The only other embarrassing moment that approaches this one in intensity also occurred due to a case of misplaced good intentions and also involved my performing in an area I should leave to others — at least in public. It happened several years ago when my older daughter was in grade four. Her teacher had arranged a talent show and she was most interested in all her students *and* their parents taking part. She told me that she understood from my daughter that I played the piano. I told her that while I had taken lessons as a child and loved to play for my own relaxation, it was hardly something I considered doing in front of an audience. She insisted that it would be good for the children to see their parents perform in such a situation and that all the parents would be doing something. So I agreed. I practised every day for my debut, selecting a little classical piece that sounded much more complicated and impressive than it actually was, and I thought it was sounding pretty good until my husband said — the morning of the performance — "You're not going to play *that*, are you?" Since I was already nervous enough — my stage fright having increased in direct proportion to every year I had been away from the stage — I decided at the last minute to substitute my classical sonata for something more accessible, and went back to *Fiddler on the Roof* for my selection of "Sunrise, Sunset." You'd think that, by now, I'd have learned not to fiddle with the Fiddler, but no, I had to be thoroughly humiliated first.

I arrived at school, music in hand, and quickly located the appropriate classroom, now filled with chairs directed towards what passed for centre stage. I was handed a program by one of the eager young students, and to my immediate horror, I noted that I was the only parent performing.

All the other names on the list belonged to my daughter and her classmates. "I'm so glad you're doing this," my daughter's teacher told me, enthusiastically. "You're the only parent who said yes." This did not make my day. As the parents began filing in and sitting down, they sent curious glances in my direction as they surveyed my name mixed with those of the fourth-graders, and I only felt worse. My nervousness increased with each individual performance. I sat numbly through songs, dances, skits, several renditions of "Twinkle, Twinkle, Little Star," and what I believe was "Three Blind Mice" on the violin, and then it was my turn. To an audience that included Shelley Peterson, the wife of the premier of Ontario — to this day, I pray the premier wasn't there as well — and writer-critic Martin Knelman, I delivered my interpretation of the classic song, and words fail to describe how truly awful I was! My hands were shaking, I couldn't find the right notes, I kept waiting — hoping? — for God to strike me dead. When it was over, I returned to my seat to a smattering of polite applause and a sea of glazed eyes. One mother whispered gently, "Don't give up your writing" as I sat down, trying to pretend I was somewhere — and someone — else. Just as I was regaining my composure, Martin Knelman, who was seated behind me, leaned forward and said, "For ten thousand dollars, I won't report this in *Toronto Life!*"

Now, he won't have to.

RETURN OF THE NATIVE

THE OCCASION WAS a festive and a generous one: fifty of Hamilton's most famous sons and daughters had been invited back to our hometown for a weekend to celebrate Ontario's 1984 Bicentennial. Our get-acquainted cocktail party had only one organizational flaw: since we were all so famous, no one had provided us with namecards, with the result that each of us spent the evening figuring out who all these other famous people were and what they had done to make them so famous.

The event everyone confessed to dreading was the Saturday morning parade in which we were all to be dragged through the streets of Hamilton, allowing less-famous citizens to puzzle over that very same question. One grace note: each of us would ride in our own chauffeur-driven vintage car, with our name (but no other hint as to our celebrity) written on a banner across the side.

A beautiful morning. No hope of rain out, despite prayer and early promise. As we positioned ourselves for collection, I noticed that my last name had been incorrectly spelled "FRAZER" on the paper banner across the side of my vintage car. At my request an official with a black crayon attempted to change the "Z" to an "S." The result: I was now "FRA8ER," spelled with an "8."

The marching bands began to play. My vintage car — a handsome cream topless with gleaming chrome — eased onto the tarmac, driven by a chauffeur, also in vintage dress. By the time we had rounded the corner onto Main Street, a few bemused Hamiltonians had begun to collect at the curb, apparently not too distressed at this interruption in their Saturday chores. Several children held balloons. A couple of popcorn carts gravitated like fleas scenting blood. One or two elderly citizens — no doubt famous persons' relatives — even had camp chairs. Though many fans could be seen pointing at us and wondering aloud who we were, all seemed good-humoured and a number waved. I waved back, just as the Queen would have handled it, even allowing myself to think: "Hey, this isn't so bad!"

Ahead was the mayor's viewing stand along with the TV cameras. Just as I preened myself for a radiant celebrity smile, I heard *sputter putt-putt-poop*. My vintage chariot collapsed and died. No amount of coaxing or cursing could get it to change its mind. I was shoved over to the side of the road while the procession of other famous people wheeled past.

One shouted in pity, "Get in my car. There's room, come on!"

As I puffed to catch up, he shouted again, "Bring your name!"

Running back to my own car, I retrieved my paper banner, then leapt in the car door now open for me. As I proceeded to stick my banner on the side of this other famous person's car, his female companion commiserated: "Oh, that's too bad. They've spelled your name wrong."

"Yes. FRA8ER — with an 8."
"No, I mean your first name."
It was then I noticed it was spelled "SLYVIA."
SLYVIA FRA8ER . . . with an 8.

ONLY ON SUNDAY

STARVATION, VIOLENT BLIZZARDS and polar bear attacks are immediate images one envisions of the ruthless Arctic. But I have found that transportation and a place to lay your head at night can present the gravest day-by-day problems.

In the early 1950s, the Central Arctic Patrol was conceived as an exciting new way for the federal government of Canada to range by air over the enormous distances in the Northwest Territories. The idea was that half a dozen persons were to visit remote settlements to check that those who had been sent out to assist the Inuit were doing their jobs. This annual adventure was planned to take place during the best, but not the warmest, weather of early spring. The patrol used a single engine aircraft, a Norseman on skis — not ski-wheel as seen today, but regular wide wooden skis.

On this particular patrol, we were piloted north from Churchill, on the west coast of Hudson Bay, by the famous Arctic bush pilot, Gunnar Ingerbritsen. (Sadly he died soon after, when his aircraft iced up and crashed along our same route north.)

48

The Norseman was a strong, stubby type of plane. With Gunnar piloting up front, it would take six more of us. There was the RCMP superintendent of the Arctic, the Anglican bishop of the Arctic, the Hudson's Bay Company head of northern stores, the superintendent of Arctic Education, the head surgeon from the Department of Health and Welfare, and myself, a northern service officer.

Beyond our own weight, we each had some small personal kit and a sleeping bag plus questionnaires. Oh, yes, we had on board as well two wooden cases of overproof rum. At least one person with us did not appreciate this extra frivolity. Most, however, thought it only sensible. After all, it would be rationed carefully over our twelve intended Arctic stops. One bottle for each Hudson's Bay host was considered the only logical gift to give as thanks and payment, when seven bodies descended on his post, hoping for food and adequate space on the floor. Besides one gift bottle for our ever changing hosts, there was another bottle for ourselves.

Now, as you might guess from the cast of characters, there were a lot of different Arctic philosophies aboard that one small rugged plane that did not always find agreement, but we packed ourselves together like childen's stuffed animals. We sat facing one another, three on either side for balance's sake, most with hairy hat flaps hanging down like the ears of cocker spaniels. Our daily plan was to fly from one small settlement to the next, land, scurry around gathering information, then eat, drink, sleep and take off again to repeat the operation in the next place on the following day. The Arctic hands we interviewed were always different; it was never boring.

The weather was murderously cold during our trip but clear for flying. Our gifts, which we called floor samples from the rum boxes, were for the first few days holding very nicely, which meant our travels were on schedule. You might think that our man from Education would have stayed with the teacher from Education, and the RCMP with the police, etc., but it rarely happened that way. We travellers, as evening came, preferred to gather together, not just to share the rum, but perhaps to see that no one bit you, your church or arm of government in the back if you were absent.

About halfway through the journey, our landing in Igloolik was very rough and caused us to tilt over quite a bit, making a long slice in the snow with one wing tip and badly banging up one ski. We seven gathered our sleeping bags and our wooden boxes and marched into Igloolik. We met a jolly Hudson's Bay man, very well known to us. Near him lived two Oblate priests who wore long black robes and sealskin boots and welcomed the chance to talk about their homes in distant France. Most Inuit were away on the spring hunt. We remained there five days before another ski could be flown in. Our wooden boxes were a whole lot lighter when we left. No matter how diverse we were in religious or political thought, we did manage to form a lovely barbershop sextet.

In those far-off days of bush flying, a number of unusual habits were acceptable that would probably not pass air regulations today. My least favourite of that time was the theory that a pilot plagued by unreliable fuel gauges could not possibly tell if a wing tank were truly empty until he actually heard it run bone-dry. The effect of this test would be that the violent roaring of the single engine Norseman would suddenly cut out — stop — go stone-dead, causing a deafening silence high above the middle of nowhere! There was always a long pause while we passengers waited, heart in mouth, to hear if the other wing tank would, please God, cut in. There we sat, facing each other, six stolid men in bulky pants and parkas. I would stare bug-eyed at the bishop, who sat across from me, and he would make a tight-lipped grimace back. As time went on, this gripping aerial test of

nerves perhaps caused some mental anguish among our little band of travellers. When we landed at Spence Bay, after
one of these overlong gas tank heart-stoppers, I noticed that
we nervously consumed twice our rum quota.

Bathurst Inlet was judged to be our last night on the
floors. Our journey was almost ended. To celebrate, we decided to polish off the rum.

We delayed our takeoff because of a scattered herd of
musk ox near our best run. It was Sunday afternoon when
we headed towards Yellowknife. It was the warmest day that
we had seen. On this final leg, only one more heart stopper
would surprise us. While we all tried to hold up the aircraft
with our stomach muscles, the bishop and I locked gazes
one last time, each hoping the other would be the first to
scream out in fright. It was a draw.

Two hours later, Gunnar started our long glide down towards Great Slave Lake through the blinding afternoon sunlight. There was a small airport at Yellowknife, but its
airstrip was cleared and not suitable for our pure ski-landing
gear. Gunnar warned us of soft wet snow and we buckled
up our seat belts and snuffed out cigarettes for the first time
on our entire journey.

Gunnar made a perfect if somewhat soggy landing. The
glaring snow around the Norseman made us want to shut
our eyes. From here on we would use commercial aircraft to
Edmonton and farther south.

"Carry only what you need into Yellowknife," Gunnar
called back to us. "We'll send a wide-track vehicle out here
at midnight, when the snow is hard, and bring your gear in
for tomorrow morning's flight. It's only about a two-mile
walk to town."

When I jumped out the rear door of the Norseman, I
plunged above my knees into clogging snow.

"You want your sleeping bags?" yelled Gunnar, who was
preparing to come staggering in with us.

"No, no! Forget the sleeping bags," said the bishop.

"Forget the baggage," I called to the others. "Just walking in is going to be tough enough."

"Bishop, you go first," I heard the surgeon cry. "It's the Sabbath and only proper that you be allowed to break trail for all of us."

It was so difficult walking that we all had to take turns breaking trail. We staggered up the bank at the edge of town and walked along the road until a kindly citizen allowed us to pile into the back of his garbage truck. He drove into Yellowknife, dropping us ingloriously in front of the hotel.

The small lobby inside the building felt sickeningly hot after our long Arctic journey. We flung open our parkas and pushed up to the front desk with a feeling of relief, yet nervousness since the cramped space was already smoke-filled and jammed with prospectors, miners, ne'er-do-wells and even a pair of young women searching for northern gold.

When the man at the hotel desk finally got around to us, he said, "Sorry, boys, there's no beds left in town tonight."

We looked at Gunnar with alarm, for we had asked him to radio ahead for rooms.

"Yeah, we got the message," the hotel clerk moaned, "but you're too damned late! It said you'd be in here by three o'clock."

He jerked his head toward the wall clock. "It's after 7:00. We've let your rooms. I mean . . . we're bloody overcrowded here!"

We could see that, but after sleeping endless nights on Hudson's Bay Company floors and suffering those heart stoppers in the air and finally the garbage truck ride, we were eager to find sleeping space under one roof, terrified that we might otherwise be forgotten in the morning.

Gunnar reeled off our credentials to the desk clerk. "This man's the bishop of the Arctic. This one here's the head of the Hudson's Bay Company. Look at this famous man —

head of the Mounted Police in the Arctic. Here's the head of Health and Welfare. This man's boss of Education. You have got the whole damned Arctic powerhouse standing right before you!"

The desk man stepped back a pace, stared at us, then shook his head. He restudied his list of rooms. "Well, you did make early reservations. Harry," he commanded, "throw those four penny-stock prospectors out of their second floor rooms unless they pay us their week's back rent right now. And that young woman with the white boots. Tell her she's got to go or we'll call in the Mounties."

Harry pushed his way boldly through the crowded lobby and quickly climbed the dark oak stairs.

"If he gets those prospectors out, you'll have two rooms with twin beds. So who's going to share the hooker's room with the double bed?"

No one raised their hands.

"Well, right there that's a problem," sighed the desk man. "Four of you can sleep in twin beds and what about the other three?"

Everyone was deadly silent.

"Tell me, how's it going to go?" He sounded tired. "You guys have got to work this out between you."

"Cut the cards," said the British surgeon gaily.

The bishop, who did not approve of cards or imbibe alcohol, gave him a glassy look.

"Have you any long wooden matches?" asked the superintendent of Education, always ready to solve any problem.

The hotel keeper pulled open his desk drawer and produced a box of matches. "Shall I break off the right number?" he asked. He then looked up and shouted at a bleary-eyed lobby bum who was eyeing our cleric's purple shirt front and stiff white collar. "Will you stop bugging that man? He's a bishop!"

First the surgeon, then the Hudson's Bay man drew short

match lengths, meaning they would share a room with twin beds. They both breathed a sigh of relief, then grinned triumphantly at the rest of us. The bishop paused, closed his eyes in prayer, then dramatically drew the first long match. He looked at the rest of us defiantly. Clearly he would have to share the double bed.

At that very moment, our pilot announced that he was bowing out of the contest, that he had just then decided to stay up all night, that he would go to the hangar and personally arrange that all our sleeping bags and gear be brought up to the airport to meet the early morning commercial flight.

The RCMP superintendent then drew a short match and so did our superintendent of Education. The bishop and I stared at each other in frantic disbelief. Could it be true? The two of us were going to sleep together.

We all signed in and the hotel man handed out the three room keys. I offered ours to the bishop, but he shook his head despondently, then shuddered, undoubtedly at the very thought of sharing the same bed with me.

We ate in the only place we could in those days. Yellowknife was not what you might call a gourmet town. Later, we trudged back to the hotel, our open sheepskin boots aflopping and our padded Arctic parkas open to the new warmth of the south. I hid nervously in the middle of our small crowd and noticed that the bishop was trailing well back in the rear. Probably he was considering whether he could ask the local Mounted Police if they had a spare private cell to accommodate him for the night.

We reentered our overheated lobby. The others yawned, looked at their watches, then leered at the bishop and at me. "Sleep tight," they called to us. As they mounted the stairs, one of them must have made a joke, for I could hear that awful sound of men of history suppressing giggles.

The bishop, dead tired like myself from all the mogging through the snow, trudged heavily upwards. I followed him limply, key in hand. When I unlocked the door, we were greeted by the smell of smoke, perfume and gin, none of which had cost a lot of money. The bed was double all right and sagged in the middle as though it had been overused.

The bishop did not speak. Indeed, he seemed to be holding his breath as he laid his black briefcase on the cigarette-burned bureau top and slowly unpacked his long nightgown.

I turned my back to avoid seeing him get into it and took off my own clothes. I had brought no kit with me save a toothbrush and a razor secreted in my parka pocket. I wished now that I had brought my unused pyjamas and not planned to sleep once more in my long, saggy-looking winter underwear.

The bishop's nightgown was snowy white and as I glanced at him, his polished steel-rimmed glasses seemed to flash a warning signal to me. Then, without a word, he knelt down on his side of our rickety double bed. He didn't close his eyes but folded his hands against his chin, prepared to pray, still staring relentlessly at me.

I could remember kneeling to pray beside my bed when I was very young, especially when one parent or the other watched me closely. But that had not happened for more than twenty years. Now, what was I going to do? Absolutely nothing, I thought, as I turned down my side of the blankets. Just because I was getting into bed with an Anglican bishop for the first time in my life was no reason for me to revise my adult lifestyle and imitate his calling.

I glanced at him again. He was still kneeling, chin propped against his fingertips, his eyes wide open, staring relentlessly at me through his icy steel-rimmed spectacles. I could feel my spirit melting.

Slowly I knelt down on the other side of the double bed. The flowered linoleum floor felt hard and cold. After a while, I heard the bishop give a true missionary's sigh of triumph.

The springs squealed as he climbed into his side of the bed and clung there while I climbed into mine. I heard him give one violent snore before I, too, fell asleep.

ROBERT HUNTER

A Total Misfit

WHEN I JOINED the summer training program in the late fifties, the RCAF's motto was still *Per ardua ad astra*, "through adversity to the stars." Mostly, by then, it was pure *ardua*. And angst and boredom.

The "training" that did take place at Station Winnipeg left me with only one skill: we'd played pool so much I was fairly good at it. I got caught a couple of times playing on the big table in the officers' mess. This led to detail, and skipping detail led to more detail.

I had erred horrendously filling out the forms to join. Under the query Hobby, I had written "writing." Bad move. I got accepted but was assigned to Clerk/Administration. Hold on here! I, the spiritual heir to Tom Corbett, was being chained to a desk with an old preelectric typewriter and cheap carbon paper and a big metal ashtray? I, who had been reading science fiction nonstop, except for what they forced on me at school since age nine, had been sentenced to fill out requisition forms?

To leave me on the ground shuffling paper was a spectacularly dumb choice for the NORAD High Command to

57

make (surely it must have been them), refusing to let me fly.

If this was how I was going to have to stand on guard for thee, I figured piss on it.

When a leading aircraftsman ordered me to get my side-burns cut and my ducktail shaved down to a crew cut, I de-cided the moment had come. Not only did I get my hair trimmed, I got it shaved off completely. As a result, the "wedgie" I'd been issued wouldn't stay on my head. It kept slipping off.

I wandered around the station grounds in my ill-fitting air force uniform, appallingly bald (proto-punk, actually), with my wedgie tucked in my belt. Since you aren't allowed to salute an officer without your proper headgear on, it was my unhappy duty to have to refuse to salute anybody. Each of-ficer I encountered naturally hated me on sight and pounced. But I had this perfect excuse: "My wedgie keeps falling off, sir, and while I have requested another size, you know how long it takes to requisition anything around here."

The new issue eventually came through, and I had to go back to saluting. You'd think that would be the end of the story, military echelons being what they are, but a bizarre accident promptly occurred.

I was sitting in the middle of a Dakota bomber's belly one afternoon, along with the rest of the class, my back against the wall, seat belt flung sloppily over my thighs, as we took off on a rare ride to the base at Portage La Prairie, just to re-mind us we were working for an air force, not an insurance company.

It was stifling hot. As the plane began to bump along, I felt a cool breath of air on the back of my neck. Then we were up, with a gasp, into the air, engines shrieking horribly. I leaned back against the wall, which snapped open like a trapdoor. dropping me overboard. My arms whipped out, fingers clutching the sides of the yawning hatch, the seat belt finally snagging around those blessedly knobby knees. Hanging there, I twisted my neck around to look down.

The tarmac was swooping by some three hundred feet below. The wind blasted my new wedgie away, taking my tie with it for good measure. It was the same sort of feeling I'd had when drowning. Complete lethargy. I took a good look around at the upside-down grainfields below, rust-coloured in the beautiful westering light. I was eventually hauled back into the plane, two guys pulling on each leg. The pilot was furious. He made me go back out to pull the latch closed, four men anchoring me. Now *that* was scary!

So once again, I didn't have an airman's hat to wear. I didn't even have a tie any longer. And, worst of all, my story was true. They all checked it out, of course. Who would believe it otherwise? Not even an officer.

An entry went into my dossier that would surface decades later in secret government files. It said, in effect: *Poor attitude towards authority.* Fair enough.

Still, they were tolerant. They kept me in through seventeen infractions of different rules, including climbing into the jet training simulator and playing around with the instruments until I had, according to the dials, reached 76,000 feet, about as high as it seemed to want to go, and then going into a straight-down power dive that almost burned out the simulator's real jet engine. What a chuckle when the spinning altimeter came up zero like a jackpot game! I surrendered to the nearest officer, but all they did was yell at me and give me more detail.

The sad story that finally got me busted was certainly not intended. It wasn't!

There was a girl in our administration class who always had the right answers. She was always the first in her seat in class, always with her homework done . . .

Out on the parade square one day I spotted a toad flopping by. I stuffed it into my shirt pocket and managed to pass inspection, despite its thrashing about. The instant the word "Dismissed!" was yelled, I galloped for the Clerk/Admin. building, arriving a full minute ahead of Miss Top-of-the-Class.

Please keep in mind I was only sixteen. I hid behind the classroom door, and as she came striding in, hair back in a bun, I reached out and pulled open the back of her shirt collar and dropped the toad.

It turned out she had some kind of aversion to the shock of a cold slimy toad landing unexpectedly between her shoulder blades. She went out of her mind. For a few seconds I laughed wildly and gleefully. Then it sank in that she was ripping her blouse off as she spazzed around on the floor.

Oh! Oh! What could I do? I had to calm her. I got down on one knee, trying to hold her still, whispering desperately, "Please, cool it, come on, don't be like this, *please*."

That was when an entire *gang* of out-of-town officers, who just happened to be taking a tour of the base, came galumphing in through the door and dragged me furiously away from my victim.

Try reasoning with these guys! I was forced to stand at attention while the officers covered my shocked, sobbing classmate with their jackets and helped her away. I tried to explain about the toad, but the toad had vanished. Too late, I noticed the window was open. It must have hopped out.

"Sure, you twisted little fiend!" sneered one of the officers. "Tell us another one!"

Armed military police with white armbands and rifles arrived. They demanded my wedgie, since prisoners aren't allowed to wear one, and naturally they didn't believe me when I said I lost it during a training flight to Portage La Prairie. I was locked in a small room and order to stay at attention.

When I shifted position cautiously after half an hour, a voice shrieked at me from nowhere, " 'Ten-SHUN!"

I was finally led to the door opening into the commanding officer's own quarters. My instructions were to march three paces forward. I did. Of course, after two paces I smacked into the CO's desk and spent the entire interview frozen awkwardly at attention with my upper torso bent forward over the desk in a permanent bowing position.

"If this was wartime, I could have you shot," he mused. The best he could under the circumstances, alas, was kick me out.

Ardua, indeed.

No Exit

IF YOU'VE EVER TRIED to make a discreet exit from a solemn cultural event without letting anyone notice you were sneaking away, you'll understand how I happened to get myself locked into a tiny hallway at the back of the Royal Ontario Museum on a Sunday afternoon.

The day began cheerily enough with the press brunch to bring the Festival of Festivals to a close. Among the prizes handed out was one to a documentary I had neglected to see during the festival. Friends at my table were helpful enough to point out there was a repeat screening of it at the ROM that afternoon.

What could be more convenient? All we had to do was walk across the street from the Four Seasons Hotel to the museum.

The only problem was that the screening was packed, and we had to settle for seats in the front row of the bowling-alley-shaped museum theatre.

A few minutes after the projection began, something in my head went *click*. Despite the prize, the film was a fairly conventional treatment of a subject with which I was already familiar; watching it seemed like a laborious exercise in being told things I already knew. I began thinking about what else I could be doing that afternoon — and decided to make a run for it.

Several people connected with the film were there and I didn't want to make a spectacle of walking out. Right beside me next to the screen was an Exit sign. I went through the door and found myself at the foot of a staircase — beyond which was a long, winding corridor.

After tramping all the way up the stairs and down the hall, I encountered a sign that warned: "Fire exit. Do not use except in emergency. Alarm will sound."

Was I about to go all the way back down the corridor and back down the stairs? No way. I'd seen these warning signs before . . . and they always turned out to be a bluff. With confidence, I ignored the warning sign, opened the door and went through.

Just as I thought: no alarm sounded. But I was now in a cell-like vestibule, with yet another door ahead of me — this one to the outside. Just one more door and I'd be free at last, free at last, free at last (to borrow a phrase from Martin Luther King).

It was when I tried to open this final door of the journey that I got a nasty surprise. It was locked. I'd have to go back. But now with mounting anxiety I found that the other door I had gone through, ignoring the alarm warning, had locked behind me. I was trapped.

I tried it a couple of times. I knocked loudly. Nothing. Panic set in. I must be miles from anyone who can hear me. It's Sunday, and it may be Tuesday before they get around to checking this part of the building.

That's when I began kicking the door furiously and screaming "Help!" at the top of my lungs. (Isn't this the point in the bad dream where you're supposed to wake up in a pool of sweat?)

What I failed to realize was that after all the climbing, twisting and turning, I was directly over the theatre where three hundred people were watching a movie — and they could hear me as clearly as if my sound effects were coming at them through a Dolby system.

Someone who had been sitting with me in the front row came to the rescue, followed a moment later by a museum security guard.

I assumed he would be ashamed that a supposed fire exit was locked. "I would appreciate it if you would open this door at once," I said snarkily.

"I'm afraid I can't do that," he replied wearily. "You'll have to go back the other way."

The true horror sank in. Not only did I have to retrace my steps, I had to walk all the way through the dark theatre while three hundred people peered and gawked at the lunatic who'd been screaming and carrying on.

Of course I planned to write a blistering letter to the ROM pointing out the folly of keeping a fire exit locked. But somehow when I got my first whiff of sunshine and fresh air, all I wanted to do was cut my losses and forget this ever happened.

R. D. LAWRENCE

A WELCOME HOME PARTY

AS A CALLOW YOUTH, I had many self-inflicted embarrassing experiences, but as age and a burgeoning ego combined to banish the blush from my cheeks and my emotions, I sailed through all manner of would-be mortifications without pause or concern.

For instance, I once unwittingly made dates with two girls for the same time, at the same place and on the same day, although neither knew the other, nor was either one aware that I was seeing them both . . . On another occasion, after having donned a brand-new shirt, I forgot to remove one of the pins from its front tail. As I strolled across the Rambla de Cataluna in Barcelona, Spain, on a warm summer afternoon accompanied by the most dignified first-date, the errant pin began to stab at a delicate, forward-facing part of my anatomy, causing me to bend double, then to stop, pull down the pants zipper and forage for the offending stabber while my companion looked aghast and *hordes* of strolling Spaniards became ribald . . . Then, too, more recently, discussing a forthcoming book with the vice-president of my publishing house in New York City, I recalled an occasion when circumstances had forced me to squat suddenly, demonstrating the action in the VP's office and doing so with such *élan* that I split my pants.

None of the above caused me the slightest discomfiture. But having now been asked to narrate the event that I would most like to forget, I find myself divided between two definitely embarrassing occurrences. One of these was set in train by forces that were outside of my doing or control; the other was entirely *mea culpa*. In the absence of a scientific device that would measure the intensity of embarrassment, I estimate that on a scale of one to ten the first probably rated eight, and the second ten, my assessment based upon the fact that I held myself blameless in the former situation. Nevertheless, and especially in view of the fact that these are the only experiences that as an adult have been able to make me uncomfortably self-conscious, I propose to describe them both in detail and to allow others to judge.

The first unforgettable event occurred during the second half of the 1960s, while I was promoting a new book in Ottawa, accompanied by my very large Alaska malamute dog, Tundra. We were to appear on a CBC television program immediately after the late Charlotte Whitton, then mayor of the capital city. Because of timing, and after I had assured all concerned that the malamute was friendly and exceptionally well behaved, Tundra and I were asked to sit next to Miss Whitton, but off camera. The dog, I had insisted, would remain beside me without interfering with the mayor's interview.

Alas, Tundra had other ideas! Two minutes into live-time questions and answers, the huge dog sprang upright, put his paws on Miss Whitton's chair and began licking her face with great affection. Miss Whitton was amused, but the producer was not. He took a step forward, glaring at Tundra, who, quick to sense hostility, glared in his turn at the producer and growled his displeasure, causing the poor man to dart behind a camera.

Miss Whitton's interview collapsed, but she and Tundra continued on camera for the allotted span. I gathered later that the "show" was a great success.

My second experience occurred during the late summer of 1973. I had just returned to Toronto after nine months studying cougar deep in the wilderness of British Columbia's Selkirk Mountains, a time during which I had not seen another human. I was still suffering from a sort of culture shock when I called my old friend Sid Adilman and his wife, Toshiko. They invited me to dinner on a given date, and I gladly accepted.

However, some days before the appointment I had met Sharon, who not long afterwards I managed to drag to the altar. Being half Spanish and having been raised in that country until my late teens, affairs of the heart have always been high on my agenda, and I was somewhat smitten and disoriented. And on the evening when I should have been visiting the Adilmans, I was dining out with Sharon.

It was not until a few days later when Sid telephoned that I realized I had missed a "Welcome Home" party where everyone but the guest of honour was present. Of course, I apologized profusely, but I feel now as I did then that my expressed regret did not excuse my faux pas. For this reason I am glad of this opportunity to tender in public my sincere regrets to Sid and Toshiko Adilman and to all those who attended my coming home party. As Sharon said when she learned of my lapse, I was a "creep"!

DISTINGUISHED PROFESSOR MEETS CAREERIST SLIMEBALL

WHEN THOSE DAMNED URQUHART girls caught me peeing in a vacant Vancouver lot when I was in Grade 3, they established a lifelong pattern of public exposure/panic hysteria/whining remorse that has stayed with me. I seemed immune from this for a long time as I built an academic career based on exposing the incompetence and self-serving venality of a variety of individuals, institutions, industries and professions. Indeed, such books as *Dying Hard*, *The Myth of Delinquency* and *Hunting Humans* were monuments to my development as an eviscerator, and clearly hinted that I myself was above such venality.

In the early 1980s, the feds began announcing enormous increases in violent crime in Newfoundland — up as much as 40 percent, they said. This "fact" seemed to be confirmed by my own experience, as I was newly given to hanging around in downtown bars and hearing hair-raising tales about late-night assaults. On the basis of this purported crime wave, I squeezed a largeish grant out of Ottawa, and our research team assembled in St. John's in the autumn of

1984. Our team's statistician was immediately lodged in the police files; and within six weeks he was back with the alarming news that there was no crime wave. What were there were changes in police jurisdictions and improvements in police record-keeping procedures, which various government agencies — for reasons best known to themselves — were retailing to the public as actual increases in crime.

All we knew was that a solicitor general's study had demonstrated that a large proportion of adults in Canadian cities, even in sleepy St. John's, were afraid of going out at night for fear of being assaulted. Thus my part of the book (eventually published as *Violence and Public Anxiety*) became a search for the culprits who were frightening the public by proclaiming a nonexistent crime wave. I focussed on our daily newspaper over the previous eleven years, and counted more than 340 occasions when an individual, profession or social agency announced a crime wave. Curiously, the police were relatively blameless; and the media, aside from a string of hysterical right-wing editorials, were responsible for considerably less than half the announcements. The vast majority of the cries came from dozens of self-serving individuals and agencies, politicians and civil servants, ideologues and professional bodies, all of whom saw by the late 1970s that stoking the fear of violence was a most expedient means of expanding their empires and increasing their public funding.

My character is not entirely free of malice, I regret to say, and I confess I was giggling at the names of individuals who were, consciously or otherwise, abusing the public for their own careerist ends. Alas, towards the very end of the research, I came across one of the largest articles in the newspaper announcing a crime wave: there, plastered across the page, was a photograph of a professor looking an awful lot like my good self, predicting a big increase in the homicide rate, at the same time as he was politicking for a largeish re-search grant to study the "crime wave." I won't mention his name — I mean, why pick on individuals? — but I can tell you that the slimeball screamed, slapped himself hard in the face and then fell off his chair. I had forgotten all about that interview, but I won't forget it now. Ever.

ROY MacGREGOR

THE FISH HAD A FIELD DAY

IN THE SUMMER OF 1983, I took a succession of ever smaller airplanes north until the jet that had left Toronto had become a creaking Beaver heading up along the coast of James Bay and then inland to isolated Lake Wawa. I was going fishing with Billy Diamond, grand chief of the James Bay Crees. We would meet for a couple of days at a camp being run now by the natives who were once the guides for other, non-native owners, and then we would proceed back along the coast to Diamond's home village of Waskaganish, where I would complete an assignment for *The Toronto Star* on what Canada's first self-government experiment had brought to the Cree Indians of northern Quebec.

This was not my first meeting with Chief Diamond. Three years earlier we had met on an island in James Bay and the results had been a cover story on native struggles in *Maclean's* magazine. We had hit it off well then and gotten together periodically whenever he came to places like Toronto or Ottawa on business. But our relationship was still far from that which, in 1989, would result in the publication of *Chief: The Fearless Vision of Billy Diamond.* We were still feeling each other out, and I naturally wanted to make a good impression.

Chief Diamond had said that the reason we had gotten along so famously the first round was that I wasn't as rattled by bush life as so many other visiting reporters had been. He put that down to a similar, if somewhat strained, background, as I was neither an Indian nor spoke Cree. But I had come from a bush background, spent my early years without running water or electricity and, given that the village I came from was in the upper Ottawa Valley, it might be argued that I also had to learn to speak English at a later date in life.

Southern reporters were a source of great amusement of the Crees, as you might well imagine, just as American tourists are the eternal butt end of an inexplicable in-joke that is shared by Canadians who live and work in tourist towns. I was determined not to be laughed at. We were going fishing and as far as I was concerned, we would be as much in my element as his. If there was one thing I prided myself on, it was on a genetic ability to convince trout they should bite down hard on a passing hook.

We arrived at the camp and the arrangements were made to head out for an early evening stroll. There were others in the camp — an NHL hockey player, several seasoned bush pilots — and when the various parties set out, every Cree in camp came down to stand, hands in pockets, watching to see what would happen. They gathered in a group of nearly twenty — cooks, guides, grandmothers, little children — at the edge of a long dock off which the children had tied a duck decoy in the hopes of convincing a real duck or two to drop down within range of their shotguns.

Chief Diamond, sitting in the middle seat of another boat, was busy rigging his line. I was in a boat with Wilf Paiement, then a star forward with the Quebec Nordiques and one of the heavyweight contenders in the tough National Hockey League. I was also ready first as, in my enthusiasm to impress, I had earlier selected the lure I would use and had already set up my rod.

As the boats began pulling away, I threw the very first cast of the fishing trip in which the boy from the city would establish forever his bush credentials. Out flew the lure in perfect grace, out in a line deliberately chosen for effect, one that would see it splash down directly in front of the assembled Cree. I would pull the first trout from under their feet. They would probably applaud.

Out went the lure, singing through the air, the line flashing fluorescent blue behind it, the eyes of the white fisherman set with a determination that would try the powers of Hemingway to convey, out, out and then — suddenly — around and around and around and around the neck of the Cree children's bobbing duck decoy.

Thirteen times it went around. I know because the Cree guide who leaned over to cut the line loose announced each one as loudly as he could shout. You didn't need to understand Cree to keep up with the numbers. The Crees on the dock howled with laughter. They pointed, as if perhaps others somehow could not know who had done it. The children put their hands over their mouths, giggling. An old lady called something out in Cree that I didn't understand and the dock assembly collapsed, clutching their guts. I looked at my new fishing partner, Wilf Paiement. He had turned his back on me and was pretending to be searching for some forgotten lure in his tackle box. I looked starboard towards Diamond's boat. All that could be seen of the grand chief of the James Bay Crees was his fishing rod sticking up in the air and shaking. He had fallen backwards off his seat and lay flat on his back on the floor of the boat, laughing so loud and hard his cheeks were covered in tears when he finally pulled himself back up into a sitting position.

The southern reporter had more than lived up to expectations.

GARRY MARCHANT

THE GIRL WITH THE CARIBBEAN CURLS

LONDON HAD ALWAYS SEEMED such a pleasant, safe place, with its polite bobbies, cheerful cabbies and barmaids that called you "luv." Such quaintness, the witty Hyde Park corner soapbox orators, nannies pushing prams along Birdcage Walk, noonday concerts in St. James's Park, Royal Horse Guards and afternoon tea. To a callow colonial, it was so refined, so gentle.

Magazine writing took me frequently to that great, regal city. The Crown and Sceptre on Great Titchfield Street was a typical busy London pub not far from Nash's All Souls' Church and BBC's Broadcast House. It was the "local" for the CBC types, who worked in the nondescript building in Little Titchfield Street around the corner. Whenever in London, I dropped by to visit old friends posted there with the corporation.

One evening I squeezed into a table crowded with producers, reporters, technicians and many people I did not recognize. The bouncy brown-skinned girl with a Cockney accent sitting next to me worked on the fringe of the theatrical, arty crowd as a designer or production assistant or something.

It was hard to place her origins. There were tight black Caribbean curls, delicate Indian subcontinent features and a sassy London wit. She was quite unlike the wholesome, fresh-faced Canadian girls I knew, but "a bit of all right," as they say over there. She seemed to know some of the radio types at the table, so it was not like meeting a stranger.

We sat for hours drinking in that loud, smoky pub, she matching me pint for pint, as my CBC friends gradually drifted off.

With the Crown and Sceptre crowd now thinned, my lively, newfound friend decided to head towards home in the East End, a place called Whitechapel. It sounded like a pleasant suburb. I was now alone, so she suggested I join her in her "local," to see a different London.

The driver frowned when she gave the address, and we stepped into the hump-backed cab. On the way over, she told me about her friends, though, East End gangster types, she claimed. "They'll cut you, they will." I trusted she was using the universal "you."

Although this Eliza's accent, at least to the untutored Canadian ear, indicated she was born within the sound of St. Mary-le-Bow's bells, the cab headed past the church on Cheapside. We drove through ever bleaker streets, past Ludgate and Wapping and the grim Western Docks, turning finally through confusing side streets into Whitechapel. It was a bleak, sinister area, not bright and alive with pedestrians as central London. Even the cabbie seemed glad to grab our pounds and drive off without stopping for another fare.

At a shabby pub, the lady introduced me to some of her friends, rough-looking types. "This 'ere's a Can-aye-jun bloke." These lean, hard thugs, all scars and faded blue tattoos, spoke a language I barely understood, but seemed amused by the colonial and "shouted" (treated) the drinks. I always liked a bit of the lowlife and felt somewhat protected by my young acquaintance.

This was different from the clean, carpeted uptown pubs, dirty linoleum floors burnt by cigarette butts and covered with matches. Brooding blacks and shifty-looking whites played darts or hunched whispering over their glasses.

For amusement my little Eliza taught me some East End gangster slang. Not that namby-pamby, music-hall Cockney rhyming slang, but the real, hard-core criminal stuff.

"Sod that for a gang of soldiers," which meant, in mild-mannered Canadian, something like the hell with that.

"There goes the 'filth,'" she said, indicating a pair of plainclothes policemen. The tough talk was amusing coming from this delicate young woman.

We were still there when the publican barked a sarcastic "Time, gentlemen" and hustled us out the door. The streets were now empty. My friend seemed a bit tipsy after our long evening's drinking, so I walked her home to a sprawling, dingy housing development. She led me through a maze of walkways and hallways to a small apartment.

I realized now that she was quite drunk, and had just sat her down on the couch when a key rattled at the door. As it swung open, she slurred, "It's me 'oosband," and passed out, face down on my lap.

Husband? She never mentioned a husband.

Through the door stepped a hulking figure in battered combat jacket and heavy boots. The sinister silhouette filled the doorway as I struggled to rise. The rag-doll body had me pinned to the corner of the sagging couch, her head bobbling on my lap.

What could I say? "Pleased to meet you," "This isn't what it seems," or "Sod that for a gang of soldiers" seemed inadequate. My Prairie upbringing hadn't prepared me for this. The hulk stood motionless while I flailed around, trapped. With the only light coming from a low-watt, overhead bulb, it was as though we were performing a lewd act on a stage in a cheap Soho porn club. The East End had seemed so friendly before.

Without a word the shape disappeared into the apartment. I finally shoved the unconscious woman away and bolted to the door, pausing briefly — very briefly — wondering if I should try to explain our innocence. Then I plunged into the shadowy warren of the housing development. Now panicked, I couldn't find my way out, stumbling through a maze of long, grimy hallways and darkened doorways, startled by a few skulking figures.

Finally, I surfaced into the cold streets and foul alleys. There wasn't a taxi in sight, the tube was long since closed. Was that the frightening fall of heavy-booted footsteps hurrying behind me? I scampered around in confusion until a brightly lit street appeared and I got my bearings. I didn't stop fleeing until I reached Piccadilly.

Next day, in the bright light of an English spring day, it all seemed amusing as I related the incident over a lunch-time pint back in the familiar West End. My London friends had a more educated perspective.

"Whitechapel? No one goes there after dark, mate. That was Jack the Ripper's home turf."

"Yes, they play for real there. That chap was going for a razor."

I return to London frequently but haven't been near Whitechapel since. And I always tread cautiously when entering the Crown and Sceptre.

W. O. MITCHELL

Interlude at La Guardia

I BELIEVE I'VE HAD more than my fair share of embarrassing experiences. I have come to realize that they don't just happen; they have an inevitable event pattern with an early beginning leading to a humiliating climax. When my sons and daughter were children, they heard me caution them many times, "See the pattern forming." For the most part the two boys did keep their eyes peeled. My daughter seems to be more like me.

My most embarrassing experience began thirty-five years before its conclusion, a seed planted when I graduated from St. Petersburg Senior High School during my Florida boyhood and adolescent years. My mother asked me what I would like for a graduation present. This was an easy one. A Cuban fellow senior, Tommy Jaipur, was a tap dancer performing on every possible occasion in or out of St. Pete High, with Malacca cane and tilted white Panama hat — or perhaps a straw boater. He had quite a staccato repertory: "East Side, West Side," "Chattanooga Choo Choo," "Shuffle off to Buffalo," "Tiptoe through the Tulips . . ." A devout springboard diver, I had no interest in tap dancing but I envied Tommy the white Palm Beach suit he wore when he performed.

"Yeah — white Palm Beach, double-breasted suit like Tommy Jaipur wears."

My mother's face showed a shade of concern. "Oh, Billy, this past year you've grown so fast, shot up." I hadn't. Just turned seventeen, I was a good head shorter than anybody else in my year, male or female. "It's a lot of money for something you could wear for maybe only half a year."

My older brother, who was by now smoking openly, said, "Even if it did still fit you, when you go to university you'd look pretty funny wearing a Palm Beach suit in Winnipeg in forty-below."

I can't remember what the hell she did give me for my graduation present, but again and again over the decades I have recalled my disappointment at not wearing a white Palm Beach, double-breasted suit up on the St. Pete High auditorium stage to receive my parchment roll behind a quarter-mile bank of blow-torching poinsettias.

That was the beginning of something that finally bloomed thirty-five years later in San Francisco, where I was involved in a documentary film. We finished shooting early in the day and I had a free afternoon before my flight to New York. I went into Frederick and Nelson's mens' wear section, and there I saw a long row of suits. They were pure and they were double-breasted, and I bought two of them. My mother had been right. They *were* expensive. One of them had a blue, the other a chocolate pin stripe. Seersucker. I decided to wear the blue striper. Before checking out of the hotel, I changed and looked at myself in the mirror and felt a rush of catharsis such as I had never experienced before.

There would be a two-hour wait in the small hold-up room in La Guardia airport before my flight to Toronto, then

on to Calgary, and half an hour before the boarding an-
nouncement I had to go to the washroom. I was alone in
there when I stepped back from the urinal, went over to the
pedestal sink to wash my hands. When I turned on the tap,
I underestimated New York water pressure; the flow hit the
basin with such force that it blew like an Alberta oil well.

Right on target: my crotch!

Seersucker is cotton and it truly does suck; instant ab-
sorption had left a dark trail down the inside of both my
thighs, and there was no way I could walk out of the men's
toilet to face all those people in that small hold-up room;
every one of them could recognize a urine stain when they
saw it. I looked for the paper towel box. There wasn't one. I
went into the single cubicle. Some guy had used up the last
square on the roll. Then I saw the blow-dryer on the wall to
the right of the pedestal sink. The snout could be rotated up
or down. I turned it up, climbed up on the basin edge to balance on one knee with the other high and out like a dog at a
fire hydrant, then directed the warm flow upwards to dry
and erase the embarrassing shadows. It was going to take
time, but it was working. I simply had to snap the dryer on
again and again and again and again and . . .

Perhaps the fifteenth time, I heard the door open behind
me. I looked back and up over my shoulder to see two fel-
lows, both with attaché cases and their mouths open under
their white cowboy hats.

"I'll be through in a moment," I said.

I was. It could have been worse; just before they'd entered, I had realized that my underwear shorts were quite
damp and had decided not to bother with them. How much
worse to have been caught with my pants at half mast.

As I boarded my Toronto flight I had to pass the same two
seated in first-class, and the one in the aisle seat nudged his
partner and pointed to me with his thumb. He did so again

when I boarded my Calgary flight. With their gabardine suits, string ties, high-heeled boots and white cowboy hats, I'm pretty sure they were soft-thighed oil patch executives, who had never forked a horse and had been in New York, mulleting for risk capital.

I was relieved that my wife, Merna, had not been with me on that trip. In time I told her about what had happened in that New York airport washroom. She laughed herself silly, kept bringing it up for the next ten years, mostly for the amusement of dinner guests. I think the last time she reminded me of it was when the secretary of the mayor of Weyburn, Saskatchewan, where I had been born and raised for the first twelve years of my life, wrote to say that they would like to erect a life-size bronze sculpture of my fictional characters, Jake and the Kid, on the south entrance to the city. That would be Government Road heading for the border and North Dakota. I said I would be honoured. Merna laughed.

Months went by before I heard from the mayor's office again. Evidently they had found out that foundry costs in Winnipeg were much higher than they had anticipated. They did not want to abandon the project though; would it be all right with me if they did just the Kid in the spring and Jake a year or two further on down the road? This time she really laughed.

"Doesn't strike me as all that funny," I said.

"Oh no — it isn't."

"Then why the hell are you laughing so hard?"

"I just thought of something."

"What?"

"They got the wrong subject for their statue. Shouldn't be Jake and the Kid."

"What should it be?"

"You," she said.

"What, you mean — me?"

"I can just see you there at the south entrance to Weyburn — the white pedestal — up on one knee, balancing on that basin with your right leg lifted up high."

I still have those seersucker suits hanging in an upstairs closet. I have worn neither of them since that afternoon in La Guardia airport twenty-three years ago.

THEY'LL DIE LAUGHING

BECAUSE MY ENTIRE LIFE has been an embarrassment both to myself and to those who have become involved with me, I find some difficulty selecting my *most* embarrassing moment. Here is one taken at random.

Early in the summer of 1943, I arrived in England to join the Hastings and Prince Edward Regiment, widely known throughout the Allied forces as The Hasty P's. My military career up to then had been fraught with rue, in part because I was cursed by the misfortune of looking about ten years younger than my actual age, which, when I joined the army in 1940, was nineteen years. In consequence of my singularly youthful appearance, nobody in authority was inclined to trust me even to let the cat out at night, while those who were nominally my underlings failed equally to take me seriously. Shortly after I was commissioned, I was unfortunate enough to overhear my colonel discussing me with the adjutant.

"What in hell are we going to *do* with Lieutenant Mowat?" the colonel asked.

"Well, sir," said the adjutant, "we can always send him

out ahead of our troops. When the enemy sees him, they'll die laughing."

The soldiers in my own platoon were no kindlier. One of them was heard to remark: "It's bloody favouritism, that's what it is! Some outfits is lucky enough to get a Newfie dawg, or a hairy goat for a mascot. And whatta *we* get? We get a bleeding babe in arms!"

Things grew worse. At Camp Borden, where I was stationed before being sent overseas, we were inspected by a visiting English pooh-bah of general's rank and vaguely royal blood. He was enjoying the hospitality of the officers' mess after the ceremony when his bulging blue eyes happened to light on me. Hauling a monocle out of his breast pocket, he stared long and hard, then turned to comment loudly to the camp commandant.

"I say, old boy, you colonials *do* hang on to traditions rather marvellously, what? *We* stopped recruiting boy soldiers back in dear old Wellington's time."

Life was no easier for me on "civvy street" in those times. Whenever I went on leave, someone was sure to mistake me for a high school cadet or, what was worse, for a boy scout. Once when I was visiting Toronto, a dear old lady sidled up to me at a busy corner and took my arm, expecting me to escort her across the street. I did so, whereupon she rewarded me with a shiny new dime. This would not have been so bad had I not been observed by a fellow lieutenant, a hulking, great slob sporting a thick black mustache who looked to be at least thirty but was actually my own age. He gleefully told the story in the mess a few days later, adding quite unnecessarily that the dear old lady had patted me on the head and gushed: "Thank you *ever* so much, you nice young thing."

By the time I joined my regiment in England, I had tried everything I could think of to prematurely age myself, but with negligible results. I had worked with grim determination to grow a mustache, but despite massage and various hair-growing formulas, it amounted to no more than a few pale-yellow hairs that could only be seen in a strong light.

One rainy afternoon we were turned out for a ceremonial parade by a singularly gung-ho major. When he got to my platoon, he halted and in a voice that could be heard all over the parade ground, shouted:

"Mister Mowat!"

"Sir?"

"What the hell is that on your upper lip?"

"Mustache . . . sir."

"Lord Jesus Christ! That's no mustache . . . It's a disgrace! A baby could grow a better crop on her pussy! Wipe it off!"

Although my military existence in England was heavily shadowed by my too-youthful appearance, this was as nothing to the pall it cast over my private life. If there was one thing more important to every young Canadian then in England than getting into action in the field of battle, it was getting into action in bed. Try as I might, and, God knows, I tried, my efforts came to naught.

At one point I fell madly in love with a CWAC (Canadian Women's Army Corps) from my own hometown in Ontario, who was currently serving as a driver with a nearby unit. She insisted that she liked me and always had, but though I panted after her for months, the best I could get from her was sisterly affection. One night, in desperation, I accused her of being frigid.

"Oh, no, Farley dear," she replied sweetly. "I just *can't* make love with *you*. It would be like incest with my little brother. And, besides, what would your mother think?"

English girls were no more amenable. The only emotions I seemed able to arouse in them were maternal ones. They would take me to their parents' homes; fuss over my food; wash my clothes; tuck me into bed and, sometimes, give me a friendly little cuddle. Beyond that they would not go.

"It wouldn't be right, luv," one of them replied in response to my urgent suggestion that we get on with it. "It'd be like robbing the cradle, so to speak. Now just you toddle off nightie-bye like a good boy."

In the spring of 1943 it became apparent that we were soon to go into battle, with the consequent certainty of bloody dissolution for some of us. That prospect did not especially terrify me, but I was double-damned if I was going to carry my virginity with me into the next world. In June we were given ten days' embarkation leave and I knew that this was it. Come what may, I intended, in the elegant metaphor of the times, to get my ashes hauled.

I headed for London, taking with me a stock of nylons and cosmetics, which my sympathetic father had sent me from Canada, together with every penny I could squeeze out of our paymaster. I was ready, and I was resolute. This time I *would* not fail!

And yet I did.

At ten o'clock on my last evening, I was pecked on the cheek in platonic farewell by a superior young lady who had been my last, best hope and upon whom I had lavished lipsticks and nylons, theatre seats and dinner at the Comedy Restaurant.

"Ta, ta, dear," she said as she slipped into the only taxi on Piccadilly Circus, and neatly closed the door upon my last entreaty. "If you get leave again, *do* come down to Rye. I mayn't be there, but Mumsy and Daddy would simply *love* to have you stay, and my dog would love you half to death."

I was not utterly alone in a cold and foggy world. Since there were no more taxis, I decided to take the underground back to my monastic hotel room. As I boarded an escalator and went clattering down into the bowels of the earth, I felt not unlike Dante descending into eternal purgatory.

Then, as I peered down into the smoky gloom of the sloping tunnel, I beheld a vision rising towards me on the equally crowded, upbound escalator. A blazing blonde with ruby lips and a roving eye, she wore a skirt and sweater so tight they melded to her skin. She was the epitome of the fabled Piccadilly Ladies whose skills, if not virtues, were extolled wherever soldiers went upon this earth. And she was unaccompanied.

In that moment I believed that the fates had at last relented. They were giving me one final opportunity. Resolutely I put out of mind the many ghastly army films dealing with the horrors of prostitution and venereal diseases that I had been forced to watch. She and I were fast approaching one another. I leaned over the moving balustrade, mustered all my strength and in a voice made unnaturally loud and shrill by my unhappy plight, made my proposal.

Everyone within earshot on both moving stairways turned his or her head towards me, and we waited for the demoiselle's reply.

She drew level with me, barely an arm's length away. I stared into her merry eyes beseechingly. She returned my earnest gaze and smiled enigmatically but did not speak. It was not until the magic stairs had carried us several yards apart that her clear voice pierced the pregnant silence that held me and the audience in thrall. I hear her still . . .

"Oh *do* run home and have your nap . . . you funny little chap."

BREAKING ICE

I WAS IN NORWAY in 1982, and went from there to Sweden. Norway reminded me a little bit of Canada as it was when I was younger. There was a feeling of propriety, a severe gentility, at odds with some natural roughneck tendencies. A lot of men on the streets of Oslo looked like dressed-up farmers — from the days when farmers were brawny from hard work, but tame and rather dazed in their Sunday clothes. Social occasions — the ones I was taken to — seemed to be exceedingly polite, and there was not much to drink. That is, not much was drunk. Two glasses of sherry, perhaps, during an evening party. When I ordered a beer one day at lunch, I detected surprise, not to say consternation. No wonder — it cost about as much as my excellent, ample meal. I soon learned that the price of liquor, and even of wine or beer, made these things almost prohibited luxuries. Some people, I was told, made their own wine or home-brew, but of course I never got any of that.

What I did get — as a present from the Canadian embassy, when I was leaving for Sweden — was a large bottle of whisky. I hardly ever drank whisky at that time, and that probably accounts for the fact that I don't exactly remember what measure of liquor this bottle contained, or whether it was Scotch or rye. (I would like to say it was rye, to make this more of a Canadian story, but I do rather think it was Scotch.) I really wondered what I was going to do with such a thing. Somebody told me that in Norway or Sweden it would cost around seventy dollars. It seemed to me a dubious present and a considerable burden.

In the hotel, in Stockholm, the doors to all the unoccupied rooms were standing open. I entered my room, 120, without having to use my key, closed the door and started to unpack. I unwrapped the bottle of whisky and set it on the coffee table. I noted that I had been given a very fine room, with twin beds and a desk and leather chairs. A good room for a writer, I thought. Most rooms don't have a desk you could imagine really working on. A particularly good room for a writer (not me) who was in the habit of calling conferences with other writers and sub-writers and idea-persons. Everybody would sit around the coffee table, smoking like mad and tossing back the whisky and crumpling paper and arguing and groaning (I had seen it in the movies) while they whomped up a play or a garbage bag commercial.

I hung up my dresses and put some things in drawers and spread out notebooks and pens and reading material. I arranged on the bathroom shelves my cosmetics and shampoo and various jars and bottles containing substances which add to or subtract from the body's natural smells, and ensure its cleanliness, softness and durability. I got into a dressing gown and began to run a bath.

There was a knock at the door. Not the timid knock of a literary fan, bringing a book to be signed (if I had such a thing as a fan in Sweden), or the cheerful knock of the hotel management offering fruit and champagne.

This was the knock that summons you to an interrogation.

Two men in their thirties, perhaps in their early forties, were standing outside. They were wearing dark, good suits and they had very short hair and glasses. They had shaved recently. Trim was the word. Their English was excellent.

"You are in our room," one of them said.

My English is excellent, too.

"Oh, no," I said. "I don't think so. I think you have made a mistake."

"No. There is no mistake. One hundred twenty."

He showed me the key.

This was a setback, but I went and got my own key, explaining pleasantly that the desk clerk must have given out two keys to the same room. I glanced at the key as I held it out for them to look at. I saw the number. 112.

"One hundred twelve."

The male voice made this observation briskly and precisely and without noticeable triumph.

Then of course I realized what had happened. I had not heard the number correctly when the clerk told it to me. And I hadn't looked at the key because I hadn't had to use it. I had noticed the size of the room and the two beds but I've often been shown to a room like that when travelling alone.

I began to explain all this. The two men entered the room with their luggage and briefcases. They took possession. I apologized. I may have laughed. I may have clapped one hand — girlishly — to my face. Oh, how embarrassing. I am sorry! I waited for them to laugh or at least smile and say never mind, quite all right.

They didn't do that. The Swedes did not think this was funny and they certainly did not think I was charming. They thought I was stupid. Now, plenty of people, in North America, would think the same. Men or women. But in North America we have a habit of covering up such feelings except with members of our own families. We give back smile for smile. Not at all, no problem, don't worry about it. Apologies and reassurances and more smiles all round. ("Christ, what an idiot," we say when the fool woman skitters off finally to her own room.)

The Swedes just stood there, in possession, unsmiling, watching me fling dresses off hangers, cosmetics off shelves. Nobody helped me carry the first load down to 112, a narrow room with no desk and a window looking directly into a room where a man was mending shoes. They allowed me to flounder, though they must have learned many useful polite phrases in their English courses. They waited — mute, stony-faced, honest. But when I came back from 112, I noticed a glimmer of interest — in fact, a look of controlled amazement — had replaced the look of calm censure on their faces.

They had spotted the whisky.

"Would you like a drink?" I said. I thought that they would curtly refuse. And indeed I saw the curt refusal rise to their lips, but not get past.

They said yes. They would. Please.

So I poured, and we stood around, then sat around, tasting the Canadians' gift. Curiosity as well as thirst had got the better of them. What kind of woman travels with provisions like this, they wondered, and finally got around to asking. A writer? Was it possible? A lady writer. But I must be very popular, they said. I must be a *very popular* lady writer.

And so on, the fragrant, expensive, extravagant booze melting the edges of glacial deportment, until one of them actually helped me carry my remaining clothes and books and toothpaste down the hall. Both bowed slightly, regretfully, as I removed the bottle on my final trip.

For once, I thought, the Canadian embassy knew what it

was doing. Maybe they had spotted me as somebody who might need this kind of help. Grain liquor, the hard stuff, reliable ambassador and mediator, temporary but expedient promoter of human kindness, soothing courtesies, a little lubricating hypocrisy, among the large pale people of the northern latitudes.

"WALTZING MATILDA"

SINGING AND HUMMING have too often got me into trouble. Normally, it's a happy pastime, but there are times when it suddenly becomes less so. I can recall being heaved out of music class in high school when my enthusiastic vocalizing was greeted less than benignly by my teacher, who felt it more like a banshee howl than a melodic baritone.

But the embarrassment of that moment was relatively minor, even if personally long lasting: only a couple of dozen fellow students were witnesses to my absence of musical talent.

The embarrassment was not minor, however, when singing overtook my normal good sense in my role as anchor for "The National" on television.

One evening we were reporting a news item from Australia on the Aussies' bicentenary celebrations, appropriately accompanied by a stirring rendition of "Waltzing Matilda." Swept up with the verve of the moment as I watched the news report from Sydney flick past on my television monitor, I quite unconsciously joined in with my own hearty rendition of "Waltzing Matilda." That would not have been a problem normally since it would only have assaulted the ears of the cameramen and the floor director who were with me in the studio. Unhappily, however, as the report was ending, the director up in the control room inadvertently (inadvertently, I think!) cut back to me in the studio, and there was I lustily ending a rousing chorus of Australia's favourite song, which was seen and heard by the entire nation. I smiled sheepishly and went on with the next news item.

But perhaps the worst on-air moment of chagrin spawned by my alleged singing came on a New Year's Eve as we were ending "The National."

New Year's Eve was the only night of the year when things were just a little looser in the newsroom as colleagues would provide cakes and cookies and I would bring in a few bottles of champagne. It was the custom to end "The National" on a light note on such occasions, and I gathered as many editors, copy clerks and technicians as I could round up, and they stood behind me around my anchor desk as the program ended. The idea was for all of us to shout out "Happy New Year!" to the country in the final ten or fifteen seconds of the program.

On this particular New Year's Eve, however, as we began this festive salutation, to my horror I heard through my earpiece a suddenly panicked script assistant say, "Oh shit! It's two minutes and fifteen seconds."

Now two minutes and fifteen seconds is an eternity on network television, especially when you have nothing with which to fill the time. With all my colleagues standing there behind me grinning and shouting "Happy New Year!" I could think of nothing to do to fill up the unexpected and unwanted extra time except to have everyone burst into "Auld Lang Syne." The trouble was, I was the only person with a microphone. The result was an exhibition of unquestionably the worst vocalizing ever inflicted on an unsuspecting nation.

In the days that followed, letters flooded in — a few misbegotten souls praising my singing, although more for the enthusiasm than for the musical quality; but most, alas, were either curious as to whether something had gone wrong with their TV sets or downright critical. A lady in Winnipeg sent me an article entitled "For the Singing Impaired." Another letter writer from Qualicum Beach, B.C., said her husband used to say she had the worst singing voice in the world, but "when you broke into song, my husband paid me a compliment by commending my voice in comparison with yours. Thank you."

These days I try hard to restrain my musical enthusiasm as my contribution to the continuing good health of Canadian eardrums.

ALAN PEARSON

THE BURNING LIGHTER

I FOUND IT ON THE PLATFORM of Liverpool station on my way to catch a train to Manchester. There it lay on the cobblestone ground, glossy black enamel with gold (not golden) trim — a genuine Cartier cigarette lighter. I picked it up, pocketed it and, full of guilt, hurried to my train. I should have turned it in to the stationmaster. After all, I didn't need it. I didn't even smoke. But, I told myself, I might miss my train, which stood nearby, steaming and hissing on the track.

This particular train was crowded and people were jostling about in the corridors. Everyone seemed to be smoking and tobacco fumes hung on the air in still layers of blue and grey. It was a cold, rainy day, so all the windows were tightly shut and it would have been a brave young man who dared to open the window by even a crack.

There was a jerk and a series of clangs and we were soon going clickety-clack along a stretch of line that ran behind the backyards of a row of slummy Liverpool terrace houses. I could feel the glossy smoothness of the Cartier lighter in the pocket of my raincoat as I lounged against the wall of the corridor. It was a luxurious artifact to idly fondle, a stylish contrast to my shabby surroundings. With an object like this, it would be a pleasure to take up smoking.

I turned my attention from the backyards sliding by the window of our speeding train and noticed, standing nearby, a young woman of such breathtaking loveliness that she might have just stepped palpitating with life, and perfume, from the glossy pages of *Vogue* magazine. She wore an immaculately tailored cream-coloured topcoat, vaguely military, with gold buttons and frogging. Perched on her head was a matching hat with a veil — and she appeared to be alone. I realized immediately that this unreachable princess, this breathing work of art, would give me something to look at on the dreary trip between Liverpool and Manchester.

Then, to my great delight, I saw her take a cigarette from a shiny leather handbag and put it between the perfect contours of her richly lacquered lips. A more perfect opportunity could scarcely have been devised.

I did it just like in the movies. I took the gleaming lighter from my pocket and, at the dead right moment, swung my arm up and flicked the lighter mechanism, certain such a finely made instrument would light on cue. It did, of course, but I had not anticipated the liberal length of the flame it would produce. I then saw the most perfect smile of a grateful woman turn to horror as my lighter flame lit the veil of the hat.

I've always had quick reflexes, so no sooner had the little tongues of flame raced through her veil than I grabbed the hat from the woman's head and crushed the flames out against the front of my gabardine raincoat. When I checked to see if the flames were well and truly out, I saw the cream-coloured hat was singed, crushed and blackened with smeary bits of burnt veil.

I scarcely had time to savour the dismay that suddenly filled me before I heard the enraged voice of this lovely woman as she berated me long and hard, not in the accent of a London debutante — as I might have expected — but in the harsh vernacular of a Liverpool hussy.

Even now, many years later, it makes me wince to recall the acute embarrassment and shame I felt as I became the focus of attention for everyone in that crowded, fetid corridor — with more than half the journey still to go.

It seemed to me this incident was a clear example of divine retributory justice. Since that time, I've never found anything of comparable value to that Cartier lighter, but I've sworn that, if I do, I'll lose no time turning it in.

JUST ANOTHER PRETTY FACE

POSSIBLY NO EXPERIENCE in life can quite compare with that of holding the advance copy of your first book, which has just arrived by courier. At that moment it is the most beautiful volume in the entire world, totally eclipsing *The Very Rich Hours of the Duke of Berry*, a Caxton Chaucer or a mere Shakespeare First Folio, all of which pale by comparison. It is a time to celebrate and carouse, to laugh and drink as the precious object is reverentially admired by others who also laugh and drink. Time hangs suspended; and, to borrow a phrase the editor has blue-pencilled from your manuscript, tomorrow will never come.

Predictably, however, tomorrow does come, bringing with it a king-sized hangover and the unsettling reminder you must now go on the road, like an old vaudeville trouper, and promote your book. Having written this novel, or collection of short stories, or treatise on Romanesque architecture, you must now get out there and convince people that their lives will be incomplete without your book on the night table.

In my case, the first book was a novel, and I was slated to begin my promotional tour in Toronto. As I have subsequently learned, interviews are generally relaxed and un-threatening. Most are prerecorded, even those for television. Often the skilfully spliced and edited product comes across more strongly than the original interview. False starts, em-barrassing pauses and all those inarticulate sounds we use to keep silence at bay end up on the cutting room floor.

Occasionally, however, the author must go on live, a situation not unlike dining in a crowded restaurant and becoming aware that all the neighbouring tables are listening in on your conversation. In my case, the very first interview turned out to be the toughest. I went live, on television, to be interviewed by a host who treated me as though, like diminutive, wrinkled E.T., I had just arrived from outer space in a pod.

I was picked up at my hotel, a nice touch, I had to admit, and driven to the studio by my publisher's publicity director, a woman I knew only slightly. She tried her very best to put me at ease, but I steadfastly refused to be reassured. In spite of her conviction that everything would be all right, I knew I would be largely at the mercy of the interviewing host. Were he not simpatico, then it would take more than my boyish charm to salvage the interview.

On our way to the guest lounge we met our host in the corridor. He wore heavy makeup, which made him look not unlike a Sunkist orange, and his disintegrating Afro was mute testimony to the impermanence of the permanent wave.

I was ushered into the makeup room, draped in a sheet and covered in orange base. I watched with alarm my trans-formation from shiny pink to matte apricot. My hair was mauled, teased, sprayed, making me look far more like an over-the-hill chorus boy than an aspiring author. I would not have bought a used car, or anything else, from the man whose reflection studied me glumly as the finishing touches were applied.

I was then escorted back to the guest lounge, where the other guests sat forlornly in a row, as if waiting for an audition they knew in advance they would fail. The notable exception was one Miss Hawaii, a pretty, overripe blonde, bursting with self-confidence. She was touring North America, she explained to anyone bothering to listen, her purpose to promote a line of royal leis, something I had heretofore associated with Charles II and Nell Gwynne. These same royal leis were fashioned of indigenous Hawaiian leaves, dipped in metal alloy and worn in a garland draped around the neck, like two fox pelts in a 1940s movie. Aside from their decorative value, they came laden with qualities of health, longevity, good luck and many other virtues I was too distracted to absorb.

A hurried consultation followed. Was the author to go on first, or Hawaii? "Let's do the author first," and I was led away, down a corridor and across a minefield of cables to the set, two nondescript chairs and a table in front of an upholstered panel, all suggesting the most aggressively bland type of suburban den. Across the studio I could see the host preparing to break for a commercial.

"And our next guest is Montreal writer Edward Phillips, who has just written a controversial novel about a hom-o-sex-ual Westmount lawyer."

My heart leaped down. To being with, I was astonished by the sleight of tongue that could stretch the world "homosexual" into four syllables. It sounded like a truly dreadful affliction, one of the plagues called down by Moses on the Egyptians. Had the voice from the Burning Bush seen fit to use that word, it would have been uttered with four syllables. Well, my good fellow, when I was a boy, men did not permanently wave their hair!

But the damage had been done. Heaven only knows what images of transvestite flamboyance the viewing audience conjured up while they were warned darkly against the dangers of wax buildup, or the advisability of spot soaking ring around the collar. During the break the host crossed to sit in the other chair, smiled nervously and fidgeted uneasily, as though he were the interviewee.

What the audience actually saw, when the camera zoomed in, was a middle-aged, Brooks Brothers, buttoned-down Wasp, with white hair and orange skin. My host began by asking one of those totally unformulated questions, the kind of question asked by someone who has read no more than the copy of the dust jacket, "Why did you write this book?" or something equally inane. But having used that controversial, four-syllable word in his introduction, he was obviously unwilling to pursue the subject further, and retreated instead into a state of on-camera catatonia. I was left stranded, a high-wire act without even a wire, let alone a net.

The upshot was that I ended up interviewing myself, and a spirited interview it turned out to be. I leaned forward, looked directly at the glazed host and improvised, just as I had years ago when I taught school. Occasionally, as I paused briefly to inhale, he would mumble a comment, perhaps even a question, totally unrelated to the novel, or even to what I had been saying. We might have been sitting on opposite sides of a sheet of Thermopane, that heavy-duty glass that permits vision but blocks temperature and sound. There was no eye contact whatsoever. Light bounced from his glasses, and during those fleeting moments when I could see his eyes, they were trained onto the tiny microphone clipped to my ultraconservative tie. Time hung suspended; and, to borrow a well-worn phrase, I believed tomorrow would never come.

After what seemed like a very long time, somebody off camera managed to catch the eye of the host, who roused himself to mutter, "Thanks for being with us, and good luck with the book."

"The pleasure was mine," I lied before I was led away. "Good luck," I whispered to Miss Hawaii, waiting to follow me on camera, her royal lei around her neck.

"Thank you, sir," she replied.

Later that afternoon I telephoned my cousin, who lives just outside Toronto and whom I had alerted about the interview.

"You were great!" he exclaimed.

"How did I sound? Did I make any sense?"

"I suppose so. I can't really remember what you said."

"How did I look — like the Great Pumpkin?"

"No, you looked just like you."

"Are you going to buy the book?"

"I already have it."

Knowing how he has boasted about not having read a book since leaving university, I did not ask what would have been the obvious question. Tomorrow had come and gone, and I did not want to push my luck.

"OH, I KNOW **THAT** ONE"

SO THERE I WAS in my rented tuxedo, sitting stiffly at the fancy table in the fancy hotel, one of a group of writers being honored at a Writers' Trust dinner, when the woman seated to my left cheerfully asked, "So, I wonder who's the writer we're supposed to be honouring at this table?"

I didn't mind the question. She was a respectable-looking sort, probably not the kind of reader who was really taken with stories about vampires, alien abductions or fun-loving serial killers who enjoyed performing brain surgery on people who were still conscious. It takes all kinds. So, I smiled back at her, straightened my snap-on rented bow tie and said, "I'm the writer who's supposed to be honoured at this table."

In screenplays they call the pause that followed a "beat." A sort of ill-defined, timeless moment in which a decision is reached, a conclusion arrived at, or the realization that the kindly old guy next door is really a blood-drinking mutant is achieved. Then, after that beat, the woman at my left smiled sweetly, as if letting me know she had gotten the joke, and said, "No, really, do you suppose it's him?" and she pointed to an agent sitting across from us who wore a much nicer tuxedo than mine.

It took three more tries over the next hour, plus two confirmations from other people at the table before the woman on my left finally accepted that, indeed, I was the writer at the table. Trouble was, she had never heard of me, and that's the source of some of the most exquisitely embarrassing moments a writer can experience. Because, the way most people not in the business see it, writers are by definition famous people. Therefore, whenever one meets a writer who *isn't* famous, well, it's a bit like recognizing a panhandler as an old school buddy. It happens, but . . . most people would rather not know about it.

Now, not being famous is a condition I've adapted to well in the past nine years of my writing career. I wasn't famous before, so it's not as if I've had to make a big adjustment. Of course, there are various levels of not being famous, some easier to deal with than others. Very rarely do I come away from checking the messages on my answering machine wondering why *Maclean's* hasn't called about doing a cover story on me. However, I am still nervous about those all-too-common introductions when the person to whom I'm being presented — usually an important book buyer, reviewer or my editor — smiles hesitantly and says to me, "I don't quite recall ever having heard of you, exactly."

Fame of Stephen King-like proportions aside, a little speck of recognition is one of the perks of being a writer and in those few situations in which an up-and-comer such as myself might cautiously expect such recognition — like at a Writers' Trust dinner or in my publisher's reception lounge — its absence can be awkward. However, as I have discovered since my encounter with the woman on my left, even a little speck of recognition has its drawbacks.

There are probably a nearly infinite number of factors that lead people to accord one particular book and its writer some recognition. For instance, there are those who remember plot. They're the ones who say, "And I really liked the big unexpected surprise twist at the end when it turns out that some of the children of the shroud were *girls!*" Usually, they say this very loudly in front of a huge group of people who haven't read the book, and now have no reason to.

There are also those people who don't remember the book as much as they remember the marketing of the book. The editor who bought my early Canadian novels for U.S. publication recalled that he had read my first novel eight years earlier. After all that time, he didn't quite remember my name. He had a hazy recollection about the title. The plot . . . well, it was something about vampires and a contract killer. But he still remembered the tag line printed on the cover word for word. Oh well, I wrote those, too.

Then there are those readers who remember absolutely nothing except the context in which they read the book. They're the ones who say, "It's been a long time since I read such and such a book and I really can't remember what it was about, but I do remember thinking at the time that I really enjoyed it, whatever it was." When I hear that, I secretly hope they can be tricked into buying the same book again and enjoying it twice as much the second time.

But finally, we come to those people who are the birthplace of embarrassment — those people who have never heard of me, never read the book, yet remember it well . . . for all the wrong reasons.

One of those people was a friend of my brother's, visiting Toronto from Vancouver. At a get-together, upon my being introduced to this friend, the inevitable words, "he's a writer," were spoken. The friend smiled hesitantly and I bravely prepared myself for "I don't quite recall, etc." But, just at that moment, my brother pulled a copy of *Bloodshift* from his bookshelf and held it up and the friend said those magical, recognition-laden words, "Oh, I know *that* one."

For one brief moment the background hum of conversation at the party fell to a respectful silence. Someone *had* heard of me after all. I had been recognized as a writer. Surely goodness and mercy would follow me all the days of my life. And then the friend kept talking and explained just how it was that she had come to know my book.

The friend had a brother in Vancouver. He was a renovator. People hired him to work on old houses and turn them into new houses. And sometimes, he'd be hired to work on houses that weren't really old but had been damaged.

One day the renovator was sent to one such damaged house. It had been rented out to a group of people who obviously believed that you can take it with you, because they had. One night they had simply disappeared, taking all the appliances, the plumbing fixtures, the light fixtures, the mirrors and broadloom, all the door hardware and even every single lightbulb in the place. Neighbours remembered seeing a U-Haul parked by the front door all night, but what's unusual or illegal about that?

So the renovator went through the gutted house to prepare an estimate for what would be required to make the place livable again. He had never seen any building so completely cleaned out. Even things that had been nailed and screwed down were gone. There was not one semiportable item left in that stripped and looted house except for a single object . . . lying in the middle of the floor . . . where it clearly could not have been accidentally overlooked.

It was about the size of a lightbulb, but a bit more rectangular.

The renovator remembered holding it in his hand, thinking about the driver of the U-Haul and how he or she must have stood in that house, late at night, just before making a clean getaway, balancing that last remaining item in one hand and a final used lightbulb in the other, knowing there was room for only one more thing in the full-to-bursting truck, and finally, after weighing all the myriad pros and cons, choosing to take the used lightbulb.

The one item that had been left behind, the one item that there was just no more room for in a giant U-Haul, was, of course, a paperback copy of *Bloodshift*.

"Oh, I know *that* one," my brother's friend said loudly for the benefit of all at the party who were falling into a respectful silence. "That's the book the crooks who took the used lightbulbs wouldn't *even steal*."

And people wonder why writers drink.

Ah well, always in pursuit of a happy ending, I can at least take comfort from two minor, though heartwarming facts: the book that was left behind – a Virgo Press paperback first edition of my first novel – is now worth a dollar and five cents more than its cover price to collectors (and I'm not even dead yet), and I can't remember the name of the woman on my left.

Oh yeah, and if there's anyone reading this out there from *Maclean's*, my number is 416-250-6086.

NANCY-GAY ROTSTEIN

AN AFTERNOON'S DIVERSION

IT HAPPENED IN THE QUASI-FOREIGN country known as England on the Friday of the first bank holiday weekend in May. On the final day of my tour to promote a book about my travel alone within the interior of China, I spurned the offer of a publicist's assistant to accompany me for the drive into the near-interior of Exeter.

I had already completed two and a half weeks of a madcap schedule that, save London, saw eight other centres slotted into two cities a day, and Scotland squashed in as a twenty-four-hour overnight.

By contrast, Exeter was to be a "day of leisure": a noonhour interview with the book review editor of *The Express and Echo*, and a 3:30 p.m. poetry reading on the campus of the University of Exeter.

"How long does it take from London to Exeter?" I asked the driver on the night before the event.

"Three and a half hours."

"Are you sure?"

"No more than that," he replied in a curt tone, as though admonishing me for asking such an ill-mannered question.

The following morning the weather was unseasonably mild. I decided to travel in sneakers and slacks, and change into an appropriate outfit closer to my destination. I felt that a "rumpled" look would not be suitable in the London area, even for a writer.

The driver picked me up at the hotel at 8:00 a.m. After meandering through M roads and their linking two-lane sisters, he assured me that we were now within forty-five minutes of our goal. He turned onto a narrow roadway that wound through thick, overgrown hedges.

I was happily absorbing the images I had long associated with the English countryside — a brown stucco house whose black-and-gold sign offered Bed and Breakfast, freshly sheared sheep rollicking in the fields, and horizons of lush greenery. However, as the car veered around a curve, a sign appended to a tree trunk proclaimed "Diversion."

The term did not prepare me for what lay ahead. In retrospect, sabotage would have been a more appropriate warning.

We now inched behind a collection of lorries with protruding heavy machinery. They had no intention of submitting to a minisedan. Nor was there an alternate laneway to offer escape.

After an hour of restraint, I ventured to ask my driver, "Is there an alternate route?"

"I don't know. I've never been here before."

"You must have been to Exeter." I felt a need to be optimistic.

"Once. Eight years ago. But I don't remember too clearly."

The silence deepened.

The hand moved beyond the two o'clock mark.

"This diversion," I said, "how much longer do you think it will last?"

"No idea. Could be miles. Could be just over the bend."

The scenery became lovelier, the grass lusher, the sheep

more playful, and the possibility of meeting with the literary editor less likely.

I arrived at the paper for my noon-hour interview more than two hours late. The book review editor whisked me into a nearby restaurant, not an ideal place for an interview as I had not had a morsel since 6:00 a.m. I could not concentrate on the editor's questions, just on the assortment of pastries that rolled seductively by in trolleys.

"Are you having afternoon tea?" I asked hopefully as the cart presented itself yet another time.

"No. But it's apparent that you are."

Hunger gnawing in my stomach, I restrained myself from eating alone during the interview and settled for merely orange juice.

After an hour, when I came out into the sunlight again, I found my driver snoozing contentedly in the car.

"Now we're off to the university," I said.

"Where's that?"

"Don't you know?"

"Not for certain from this location."

"But we're in the town centre. Why don't we ask someone?" I nudged gently, not wishing to ruffle his pride again.

"Not necessary," he said, his car already in first gear. "British colleges are always outside the city."

We rimmed the city for an interminable length of time. After circling more green fields and rollicking sheep, we found ourselves a stone's throw away from our original destination: the newspaper office.

The sun was beginning to set by the time we ascended a winding slope towards a series of stately buildings.

"Lovely place this, isn't it?" he commented.

We drove from one ivy-covered building to another as I tried desperately to decipher the ancient lettering.

On what must have been his third go-around, the driver pulled up before a structure that bore no identification.

"How do you know this is it?" I asked cautiously.

"There's a gentleman there who's been pacing the quarter hour. He must be for you."

Within minutes I was ushered up a cluster of steps, through a corridor and into a large room with seats arranged in concentric circles. Every chair was occupied except for one.

All eyes followed me as I crouched on the squat chair, which I felt sure was designed for a miniature medieval monk.

From my indelicate position I viewed the stern throng, made up of doctoral candidates and the faculty.

"You mustn't start yet," gasped my chaperon. "Professor Wood is to give the introduction. He retired to his office pending news of your arrival."

When my turn came at last, I tried to be cheerful. "We set off from London around daybreak," I said. "I was enjoying your beautiful countryside when we came to a sign which read 'Diversion' . . ."

I looked at the faces all around me and I knew there was no escape.

BARKING UP THE WRONG CANOE

IT IS ONE OF THE UNAVOIDABLE hazards of the author's tour —
book flogging, in plain English — that the author will come
up against interviewers who have never read his or her
book, don't want to and wouldn't have time to, even if the
care were present. This is not, the A. recognizes, the I.'s
fault. If publishers insist on bringing out several dozen new
books within a five-week period in the autumn, as they do,
it follows as night does day that the book flog will be accompanied by a certain amount of creative ignorance. You get
used to the I. hastily grabbing the book jacket and plumbing
its overflowing adjectives for material on which to base his
questions.

It was thus with an uplifted heart and a smile of surprise
that I entered the small radio station in a suburban mall in
Saskatoon one crisp autumn day, to discover that the I. had
not only read the book, but had made extensive notes on it.
He had, I could see, a foolscap pad in front of him with
what looked to be about twenty-three penetrating questions.
Well, not so much questions, as comments. In common
with most journalists, I can read upside down — it comes

from hours of standing on the other side of a chase in a newsroom — and I could see that the first question to be fired across my bows was a comment, "Quite a char." I would be met with the charge, it seemed, of being quite a character. This puzzled me a little — those nearest and dearest to me do not consider me to be quite a char.; dull as bloody d.water being the consensus — but if the I. wanted character, I was prepared to fizz like a seltzer bottle.

The red light on the control console went on and, after about three minutes of drivel to which I paid no attention whatsoever, the I. leaned into his microphone and asked his first questions.

"This Tom Thomson, he was quite a character," said the I.

"So I understand," I replied. I wondered briefly how the hell Tom Thomson came into it, but perhaps he, like myself, was rich in eccentricities.

There was a pause — the I. seemed to expect something more from me, but when it was not forthcoming, he plunged on.

"Wasn't there something funny about his death?"

"Yes," I replied, "he died mysteriously. Some say he was murdered, some that he stood up to pee in his canoe, slipped, conked his head and drowned. Say," I went on, "why are you asking me about Tom Thomson?"

The I. gulped seven times in rapid succession. "Isn't your book about him? Aren't you Harold Town?"

The answers were no and no. The I. had read a book, all right, but it wasn't my book, which dealt with labour strikes and didn't come within a country mile of the Group of Seven. Harold Town had coauthored a fine book about Thomson, and I held out the promise to the I. that Town was probably just a couple of days behind me down the flogging trail, but he did not seem to take comfort from this.

"We're here until eleven," he told me bleakly and added, "What are we going to do?"

"Carry on, old son," I told him. "They can't intimidate us."

But I was not sanguine. The time allotted to our interview — this was an open-line show, you understand — was ninety minutes. Or, to put it another way, sixteen days.

The good folks out there in radio-land had been told to brace themselves for the treat, and to have all their questions ready to ask about the Group of Seven — of which Tom Thomson was not, and this was one of the few things I knew about him, a member (he died before the group was formed officially). There was a certain surliness in the air when, every time someone would ask something about A. Y. Jackson or Arthur Lismer or one of the rest of the gang, I would reply that one thing you had to admire about A. Y. Jackson or Arthur Lismer or whoever was that he never went on strike, which was more than you could say about those bums over at the post office. I would then veer off into about seven minutes of ripe stuff on postal strikes. This did not go well. I guess the folks had worked up some pretty good stuff about painting and it ticked them off, for some reason, to get switched over onto labour relations.

By the time the old clock on the wall had edged its way towards eleven, I was getting a little feverish, and if you want to say I was babbling, feel free. But at least I hung in there better than the I. We lost him about the six-minute mark. He threw his notes in the air and devoted himself to twiddling knobs and interrupting for commercials while I carried on.

And he acted downright rude when, at the end, I offered to sign Harold Town's book for him.

THE MIDNIGHT PROWLER

I'M BEWILDERED EVERY TIME I wake up in the darkness of a hotel room at night.

In confusion I wonder. Is this my own bedroom? Am I still home? Or am I visiting friends? Or have we reached our vacation destination?

Groping in vain for the flashlight on my side table, I start stumbling out of bed anyway because my wife gives me "water pills" and they leave a person no choice.

A moment later I feel the glare of the flashlight on me, and my wife's anguished voice:

"What are your doing?"

"I'm going to the bathroom."

"*That's* not the bathroom. That's the clothes closet. Now get out of there!"

I feel my way along the wall to another doorway.

"Keep on going!" orders the voice. "That's a luggage closet."

The next door — I hurry to grab it before it can get away — luckily turns out to be the bathroom.

Fortunately, my wife had an inspiration the night we

spent at the grand old resort hotel, the Algonquin, in St. Andrews, New Brunswick. I was there as the speaker at the annual convention of the Chemical Producers of Canada. The program concluded with a dance, and we returned tired to our room to turn in before midnight.

"It's simple," my wife said happily. "Just open the bathroom door a crack, like this, leaving a glimmer of light under it. When you see the light, walk in."

I thanked her and rolled into bed. It was a warm night and I was wearing only my pyjama top.

About an hour later I awoke with a start, hastened to the door with the light shining under it, went in, shut the door behind me — and found myself in the long curving hallway, locked out of my room.

I shook the doorknob, knocked on the door, then pounded on it. There was no sign my wife could hear me.

Worse, far down the hall, still out of sight, I could hear laughing banter approaching — several couples were returning late from the dance.

I resorted to the only idea I could think of — getting down low on my knees and slowly bumping my forehead on the carpet. They might think I was a member of a new California worshipping cult.

Suddenly our door opened and I was yanked back into the bedroom.

"*What* were you doing out in the hall?"

"I was going to go to the bathroom."

"And I thought you were sound asleep in your bed. I phoned hotel security and reported a stranger trying to break into my room."

"Well, when they come, just smile and say, 'Everything's all right now.'"

"No, they'll think I liked the prowler I got. You tell them you're my husband."

When I later recounted my experience to a group, one

distinguished and motherly lady thought about it for some time and then said, "I can sympathize because I wear only tops, too, in hot weather. But didn't you realize you could have taken off the top and just tied it around your waist like a sarong? That's what I would have done."

If she was thinking of my predicament, she was right, of course. It would have simplified everything. I just didn't think fast enough.

But if she was referring to herself, the California cult might have attracted a lot of interested new recruits.

COMMON GROUND

IN THE FALL OF 1972 we moved to Oxford where we rented a house on the Banbury Road from a couple who had recently bought a newer house with gardens that backed onto the River Isis.

It was a golden year. Our house was sunny, warm and dry, and it had two bathrooms, altogether an extraordinary find in England, and the owners did everything they could to make us comfortable and to introduce us to the community life of North Oxford. After we were settled in, they invited us to tea, and on a glorious Sunday afternoon in October we walked over to their house.

Their new house seemed less attractive than the one they had rented to us, except that it had the huge advantage, very important to them, that the lawn behind the house ran down to a boathouse where they kept a punt. A nephew was visiting them from Australia, and he offered to take our two young daughters punting on the river while we had tea. Our landlord was Australian, a man in his late sixties, and while my wife talked gardens with our hostess, he and I ate cake and chatted in the living room. He was an enormously friendly man who worked hard at conversation, but we had trouble finding some common ground. Because I was from Canada, he tried to talk about the Portuguese White Fleet, the famous cod fishermen who visit Newfoundland every year, but I had not then heard of them, so we searched for another topic. All the time I had the uneasy feeling that he was waiting for me to raise an obvious subject, and then he discovered that I taught English for a living, and he pointed upwards. "What about him, then?" he asked. He was referring, not to God, but to a giant portrait on the wall above his head. I was a bit disconcerted by the Dickensian gesture and didn't immediately realize what he was talking about. "Old Joseph," he said. I still didn't realize what was going on until he helped me out again. "Conrad," he said. Of course. The famous portrait. My landlord wanted to talk about his own literary enthusiasm.

Once my eyes had cleared, we had a chat about Conrad, of whom he had read and reread every word, but I held my own better than I usually do in such circumstances. (Every English teacher has to put up with being buttonholed at parties by people, usually older people, who assume you will be familiar with their passion, and too often you have barely heard of them. "Mary Webb," they will say. "Don't you think she was the finest novelist of her day?" If you confess you haven't read the author in question, you let yourself in for a lecture. A professor at the University of Manitoba, when asked if he had read so-and-so, used to reply, "Have I read her? I haven't even taught her," but he said it one day to the department head's mother and he never did get tenure.)

I had read enough Conrad, so we were able to keep going through two kinds of cake and three refills of tea. I still had the feeling, though, that I was missing the centre of his interest in Conrad, and then when we turned to Conrad's life I found it. It was Conrad the seaman that my landlord cared so passionately about, and having established that, I launched into an account of a recent experience I had had with sailing. Before we left Toronto I had written two half-hour segments of "The Nature of Things," one on sailing and the other on over-population. (In case anyone should think that I am boasting here, referring lightly to my other talents, this is the place to say that the reason I wrote no more is because the "sailing" script was a mess, repaired at the last minute by Lister Sinclair. There.) In the course of writing the script on sailing, I had learned a great deal in a superficial way about aerodynamics, its application both to hulls and sails, and I understood thoroughly the differences between fore-and-aft rigs, square rigs and the stages in between, like dhows. Having located his interest, I lectured my landlord for about twenty minutes on my new knowledge, taking particular care to make sure he understood that with a fore-and-aft rig you needed the wind at right angles for best effect, something the team on "The Nature of Things," for all their learning, found hard to believe. Half an hour later I was just finishing off a little lecture on the story of the Clipper ships when the women reappeared from the garden. "My dear," our host said. "Mr. Wright has just been telling me all about sailing. He's been writing about it in Canada. All about the old square-riggers and stuff like that. It's very interesting." I don't know what she replied, but we moved on to other things, and soon it was time to leave.

We gathered up the children and said goodbye to our landlord. Our hostess accompanied us to the front gate where, before we said goodbye, my wife made all the connections and asked the fatal question. "Am I right in thinking that your husband is Alan Villiers?" she asked. "Yes, he is," our landlady replied. "It was nice for him to have someone to talk about Conrad with. He doesn't get out of the house much."

"And who is Alan Villiers?" I asked on the way home and

she told me. Alan Villiers. The man who had captained the replica of *The Mayflower* across the Atlantic Ocean in 1957; one of the last men to have sailed in a Clipper ship, from Australia to England; the man who captained the ships that were made for the movies *Billy Budd* and *Moby Dick*; arguably the greatest living authority on square-rigged sailing of the age; the man to whom I had just explained the difference between square-rigged ships and those with a fore-and-aft rig.

MORTIFICATION ON THE PROMO TRAIL

WHEN WRITERS POWWOW it isn't long before the subject of promotion tours comes up. But a promotion tour to flog a new book is hardly a subject; more like a verb. It's so active. You're never in one place long enough to be a subject. And, despite desperate illusions to the contrary, you — the author — aren't very important, either. The *subject* of a TV talk show is the host, as he is bound to let you know within moments of entering his sound stage. You, the writer, are the object of the enterprise, and, not unusually, the object of scorn: your sports jacket is cheap and rumpled — you only bought it for promotional purposes (it says so right on the statement you included in your expense account to Revenue Canada). Your hair is rumpled, too, but at least it's your own, which is more than the talk-show host can say. You fortify yourself: "He bought that hair," but it doesn't change the fact that he looks great on the monitor and you look like . . . well . . . like *you* — rumpled and far from home. Object indeed! Clutching your quaint, little, print-medium artifact you feel scarcely more than an article in the grammar of the promotion game.

There you are on daytime TV, tipping your novel so that it won't catch the glare of the lights, so that the viewer at home will be able to see the title, write it out immediately, rush to the nearest bookstore and purchase a few dozen copies for Christmas presents. Occasionally, when you go on a book tour, bookstores do actually have your title in stock. So you're sitting there on the set thinking how those bright lights are picking up the stain on your shirtfront from the Veal Parmesan they gave you an hour earlier on the flight from Vancouver. Or was it chicken? Or was it Edmonton?

Then there was the time on Margaret Trudeau's daytime talk show when you shared the spotlight with the Anglican archbishop of the North and the San Diego Chicken. And that live radio show at the end of the same tour when you stopped midway through your response, not knowing anymore what you had been talking about, where you were, who you were . . .

Sometimes you're saved from all the palaver. There is always the chance that your neatly typed schedule doesn't quite match up with the schedules the publisher's representatives have (i.e., Control Central has got you in Calgary the day the rep expects you in Edmonton and vice versa and so on). They always find something to do with you. Take you out for a very long lunch, or to some impressively high building; better still — out to the warehouse to sign copies of your book; "every signed book is a sold book," the rep tells you. Sometimes the warehouse even has the books in stock.

Then there're the bookstore signings. It's always the weather that explains the complete absence of anyone in the store. Well, not complete, there's always some strange soul hanging around at the end of the aisle in a filthy trench coat who eventually comes closer, drawn by the smile you have summoned up from some deep reservoir of human pity like a cur to a piece of meat. He, the cur, can't afford to buy your book but would consider it a great honour if you'd read his 960-page novel, which he has been working on for seven years and which is the greatest novel ever written, being a minute study of the every movement of an ordinary man. And he doesn't mind waiting. The store owner gets rid of the cur, but now that you aren't frightened anymore he can see that you are feeling pretty small. He makes you feel better by saying encouraging things like, "It's weird, you know, usually the store is packed at this time of day." Then he recalls with a sigh the lineups they had for Sophia Loren. Maybe, you think to yourself, if I'd written something with a bit more décolletage . . .

One seasoned pro of the promo trail told me he insisted there be a forty-ouncer of Scotch in every hotel room. A little something to take the sting out of the excruciations. A little something to smooth out the rumpled ego. You could go to the bar but somebody might ask you what you do; somebody, maybe, who is in town for a waste disposal management conference. "Hey," he says, "a writer, huh? Would I know anything of yours?" To which you might answer, in your cups, "Probably not. Do I know anything of yours?" But what kind of promotion is that! You're out there to meet people, knock 'em dead. The irony of it all is that while you are in the act, ostensibly, of becoming a "household name," you realize at last and painfully the profound depth of your insignificance. Nobody has the foggiest idea who you are.

This, I have sometimes thought, might be the real reason publishers send you off on these all-expenses-paid excursions into the ether; you come back beaten, so much putty in their hands. A pushover when it comes to negotiating your next contract.

I know what you're thinking. Listen to this guy complain. Jeez, I'd give my eyeteeth for a week or two of glamour —

away from the kids, meeting important celebrities like Margaret Trudeau and the San Diego Chicken, staying in hotels . . .

There was this hotel. Cowboys stayed there. There was no wake-up service, just a radio. I could set it for bird songs, AM/FM or the alarm. I turned and pushed and pulled and slid what I prayed were the appropriate dials and knobs, turned off the light and descended into that which passes for sleep on the promo trail in a hotel frequented by cowboys. I woke up in the pitch black to the alarm. I could have sworn I'd chosen bird songs. I lashed out at the noise, groped for the radio, thumped on the cruel knobs. I succeeded only in turning on the vibrator, operated, I learned at that moment, by this most malevolent of radios. But I could not stop the noise. There I was, vaguely conscious, massaged pneumatically by invisible fingers while my ears were assaulted by this claxon: too shrill for a radio alarm and mystifyingly seeming to emanate from the hall? Mercifully the vibrator, turned up to max, bounced me clear out of bed. And in a state of full consciousness bordering on delirium, I stumbled to the door. So did nearly everybody else on my floor. I apologized. I needn't have. It seemed the hotel was on fire. I put on shoes and a rumpled sports jacket over my pyjamas and joined the other guests shivering in the parking lot.

Some cowboy had set his bed on fire. The firemen would have it under control in an hour or so. I noticed with some satisfaction that my state of dishabille was about average. Apparently, cowboys on the trail don't take along bathrobes either. I wouldn't have minded a hat, though. It started to snow. I looked up at my room. In about three hours, at six-thirty to be precise, someone from the local rag was coming around for breakfast and an interview. I wondered if I would be able to turn the vibrator off by then. Hi ho the glamorous life.

OK, OK, you say; a little ego bashing, some self-doubt, a bit of discomfort — but *mutilation*? Surely you are indulging in artistic licence, hyperbole, an annoying but understandable side effect of your line of work. I hyperbolize not. I speak of sharp objects piercing the flesh. In my case it was not supposedly a part of a ritual scarification. I only half believe that. I think it was a rite of initiation. It happened after all on my very first promotion tour.

I had just won the Seal First Novel Award for *Odd's End*. I was about to hit all the major cities promoting it. A writer friend had led me to think it would be a better than average tour — some of the interviewers I would meet might actually have read the book, he assured me. Maybe even some of the reviewers. (There was one radio station, by the way, where a courier arrived with my novel while I sat in the waiting room. The interviewer did me the courtesy of not pretending to have read it. He asked insightful questions like this: "A startling book, but did you, Tim, achieve what you set out to with this memorable opening line, 'The problem with yardlights is that they go out'?")

The day began not badly with the "Bob McLean Show" in Toronto. Bob was fine. I didn't embarrass myself, at least not on camera. I did rather deeply agitate the wonderful actor/singer Len Cariou by nattering away to him nervously in the dressing room about the show he was starring in at the time, a performance I'd seen the previous week — *Macbeth*. I should have known, well actually I *did* know, being married to an actress myself, that it is an accursed breach of theatrical etiquette, not to mention extremely unlucky, to so much as whisper the name of the Scottish play backstage — but hey, you can't remember everything.

I then flew off to Winnipeg. I was to stay at the Fort Garry. Lovely. There was even a little calling card leaning against the door to my room saying the CoCo's Escort Service could make my stay even more pleasurable. But there wouldn't be time to find out. I hadn't been there more than ten minutes, was just contemplating a hot shower and a ball game on the tube when the phone rang. It was Michael Enright from the CBC. He was down in the lobby and could he come right up for our scheduled interview? Of course, I told him. I hung up and opened the envelope from my rep I had received when I checked in telling me about the interview with Michael Enright. Oh well, thinks I, no rest for the wicked and this is why I'm here and who cares about the World Series anyway. Michael arrived and was very nice. We considered phoning CoCo, but he wasn't sure he had enough tape in his Nagra for anything more than an interview. Then he said, with a twinkle in his eye, "When I phoned was that the baseball game I heard in the background?" I told him it was. In short order he had phoned room service for a couple of Heineken and we found ourselves parked in front of the telly watching the game as chummy as can be. He was clever, insightful — and not just about baseball. We squeezed in an interview during the commercials. He *had* read the book. He seemed not to have seriously disliked it. This, I thought, is the life. What a breeze. My first engagement on the road and a humdinger. I went to bed feeling pretty good and thinking "bring on the rest of the tour."

I should have known my luck could not hold out. The next morning, bright and early, my rep drove me to a local independent TV station. There was no green room, so I didn't have to worry about offending any of the other guests. It didn't, however, seem as if there were any other guests. There was no studio audience. Not much in the way of staff, either. No makeup lady — no makeup. One camera.

The set was TV homey: an ultramodern kitchen, casual dining area and a cozy yet effortlessly chic lounge, complete with plaid easy chairs. It looked as if they'd got the local tech school students to build it.

Then I saw the host. Nobody had to say he was the host: his hair said it for him. In fact, if you had never seen this man before and ran into him walking down the street you'd say, "Look at that hair. That man must be a TV talk-show host on an independent station."

He was pleasant enough, didn't smirk too much at my clothes. He had a kind of studied easygoingness to him. His demeanour, his suit and his hair made a statement, "I'm God's Gift to Women, but I can handle it."

There was another guest. She was a little bit late, a little bit flustered. She was from the Pig Marketing Board. She was going to prepare recipes for quick back-to-school hot lunches. I was going on first, but the idea was that I would hang around and at the end of the show we'd sit down with God's Gift to Women in the cute little dining area. There, I would sign a copy of *Odd's End* for the lady from the Pig Marketing Board, and she would feed me one of her quick back-to-school hot lunches. I didn't bother saying anything about being kosher. I'm not, of course, not being Jewish, but the idea did occur to me. If only I had followed it up.

I won't bother telling you about the interview, but if I had meant mutilation above only in a metaphorical sense, I suppose this interview came close to being that. My host maimed the English language and hobbled and nobbled what little art of fiction I might claim by asking me inane questions that I could only snub or answer inanely. I decided to be chummy and so as not to appear a snob to smile a lot and just be stupid and idiotic. To his credit, God's Gift to Women was not trying to be fatuous. Like the effortlessly chic plaid easy chairs in which we sat, he came by fatuity honestly. It probably has something to do with the protein balance in his hair. This, too, will pass, I reminded myself. Then all I would have to do was wait for the Pig Marketing Lady to do her bit and "share with her" in the cute little nook.

I watched her in the ultramodern kitchen. I wondered which item I would have to taste, smile and, mouth full, nod and murmur, Yum, yum. I thought about trichinosis — who knows how long the pork had been sitting around under the studio lights! I considered Judaism.

The time came. We huddled into the nook together. God's Gift to Women seemed particularly pleased that I would be giving *Odd's End* to the Pig Marketing Lady; perhaps he was worried that he just didn't have space in his bachelor pad to squeeze in one more volume of fiction. The Pig Marketing Lady was most polite. She didn't read much in the way of mysteries, but she allowed that it was never to late to start. Then the cameraman gave us the countdown: five, four, three, two, one — and there we all were, the three of us, chuckling and looking as if we'd been having a helluva time while the viewers only got to watch commercials. I signed over the book and the Pig Marketing Lady handed me over a plate with the most curious of her lunch-time inventions for school kids: Bacon Surprise — a kaiser roll, with a processed cheese slice inside and bacon strips wrapped around the outside of the roll and held in place with toothpicks. Many of them. This had then been broiled until the cheese had melted and the bacon was juicy.

Watching her prepare this dish earlier, it had occurred to me that toothpicks in children's sandwiches seemed unnecessarily problematic. But then if you were putting the bacon on the outside of the sandwich, the toothpicks were *de rigueur*. I could see that. She had, however, made a point of warning her viewers to take out the toothpicks before serving the sandwiches.

I wonder why she forgot to take the toothpicks out of mine.

The cameraman swung around to record the Pig Marketing Lady's response to receiving her autographed copy of *Odd's End* and then swung back to record my response as I bit into the inside-out Bacon Surprise.

There was only one forgotten toothpick, actually. As I took a man-sized bite, the better to show my delight, the toothpick went straight up, straight into my soft palate, burying itself a full centimetre into the muscular tissue there. I gagged.

The cameraman seeing my face turn blue quickly swung away to the Pig Marketing Lady. Her face, of course, had turned bright red, for by then God's Gift to Women was pounding me on the back and bits of Bacon Surprise were flying out all over the cozy nook. The director cut and the show went to another commercial break. Having cleared my mouth of the sandwich, the vehicle of my torture, I was able to grab the little wooden spear itself and yank it out. The bleeding was not profuse.

I survived. I lived to tour again. It gets easier. I've become somewhat of a seasoned pro, myself. I wear a bib on airplanes and I know that if you're in Calgary and you should be in Edmonton there are early morning flights to downtown. Talk-show hosts seldom have to check their cue cards more than once or twice to remember who I am nowadays. And increasingly I find they have read my stuff. I don't think this is only because I write books for preschool-age children.

And now, if I ever forget I am a writer, all I have to do is run my tongue over my soft palate to recall the ceremony of my initiation to the ranks. The mutilation there is my cicatrix, my mark of honour. For you're not a writer these days until you've been on a TV talk show. At least, you're not one anybody knows about out on the promo trail.

FOTHING AT THE MOUTH

I REMEMBER MY MOST HUMILIATING moment in public almost as if it were yesterday. It was "Politics and the Pen," the Writer's Development Trust's Great Literary Dinner Party held in Ottawa at the Chateau Laurier on January 25, 1989. I had been chosen as the Great Literary Dinner Party's main speaker by Edith Cody Rice, a distinguished CBC lawyer, and her fellow committee members responsible for the dinner. The master of ceremonies was to be Peter Gzowski, the thinking man's Donohue, and the fulfiller, all by himself, of the ethnic quotient on "Morningside." Gzowski, I was sure, was bound to make me feel warm and welcome. There was also the Royal Canadian Air Farce for added levity — and an excellent backup in case I failed lamentably and fell on my ass.

This may come as a surprise to my readers, but I am not a fan of public speaking. Perhaps it was because my bar mitzvah speech was a legend in Winnipeg North. I so fired up one hundred old-timers in the Beth Yakov Synagogue who listened to my speech that they (average age seventy) all volunteered to fight for the Jews in Palestine.

Perhaps it was because health problems continually plagued me and sapped my confidence; perhaps it was because I only loved to perform in front of audiences that I know and who know me; perhaps because of all those reasons I had not made a public speech in a long, long time and had turned down many offers to do so.

I accepted Edith Cody Rice's offer for two reasons. I had received an offer from Stoddart to publish *Scorpions for Sale*, an offer with a big advance, and I wanted an opportunity to publicize my book. The Writers' Development Trust dinner seemed to me a natural opportunity, where, say, the annual dinner of the World Anti-Bolshevik Congress would not be.

I had already survived major surgery in my colon. I had accepted Cody Rice's offer when I was diagnosed as needing further surgery. I was to go into Mount Sinai Hospital in Toronto for that surgery three days after the Ottawa dinner speech. (Relax, my readers, my surgery was successful; as bona fide proof of my good health, I am writing this memoir standing up.) I had thought of cancelling the Ottawa engagement but I also thought to myself — fuck it — working on the speech for the dinner itself, all that would keep my mind off Dr. Slice's second go at my asshole.

At this juncture, I hasten to point out, I did not broadcast bulletins about my health to the world at large or to my fellow media titans and midgets. The grapevine did that job. From Barbara Frum up and down everyone seemed to know of my health problems; some sought my advice, others prostrated themselves before me and rubbed my nose for luck — their luck, of course, not mine. Everyone knew about me and my condition except, it seemed, the ebullient, cherubic, perpetually flushed-faced ace investigative reporter and columnist, Allan Fotheringham.

Fotheringham is, of course, the thinking man's Geraldo Rivera. At age fifty-nine Fotheringham is the *youngest* member of the "Front Page Challenge" panel, the only TV show

that is broadcast from an oxygen tent. Fotheringham's ignorance of my health condition was to cause him some embarrassment and a bit of hand-wringing; some time after the
dinner the Foth sent me a hail-fellow-well-meant letter of
apology — well, sort of an apology. If I didn't have a premo-
nition of disaster ahead at the Writers' Development Trust
dinner when I took the train to Ottawa with my wife and
daughter, I should have. Accompanying us on the train trip
was my good friend Norman Snider, freelance writer, Gemini
award winner for best screenplay (*Dead Ringers*) and a
trends interpreter. Norman is also a world master at para-
graphing and the non-use of journalistic terms in fiction.
Snider is the kind of friend that often makes you prefer enemies. Snider always tells the truth — like telling you his
mother had died from chemotherapy when you had just
started on chemotherapy. Conversely, Norman just loves it
when you white-lie about his articles and insights. Norman
had just done the cover story in *Saturday Night*: "Dark
Kingdom" it was called. I thought it was about *le roi nègre* —
the black king of Quebec. I was relieved to find out it was
about Brian Mulroney and contained the odd insight of
mine that Norman was kind enough to borrow. Anyway,
Norman and I passed the time away on the train talking
about his articles and screenplay — and related subjects,
like Norman's animus for Robert Fulford, the editor of my
book *Scorpions for Sale*, and one of my best friends.

At the cocktail hour before the Ottawa Writers' Development dinner actually began, I bumped into virtually over a
hundred people I knew well from the writing and media
world. I was calm and happy and eager to do my stuff. My
stuff would be a very short speech of less than fifteen minutes. I would read a story from *Scorpions for Sale*. My allotted time was twenty to twenty-five minutes. I surmised that
no one would be hung from the ceiling if I hit thirty. This

had all been cleared with the dinner wagon master, Edith Cody Rice.

Things at the dinner were going so well that I was signing autographs in old remaindered books of mine — gladly and joyously. I even listened empathetically to the inanities that flowed from the lips of Margo Roston, my neighbour at the *Ottawa Citizen* table I was sitting at. Margo is the kind of Ottawa Jewish answer to Zena Cherry. Margo's father, a Lawrence Freiman, owned Freiman's department store in Ottawa and was a good friend of Mackenzie King. Indeed, the Freimans made legitimate Mackenzie King's claim that some of his best friends were Jewish.

My first hint of trouble ahead was Gzowski's interminable speech of about forty-five minutes. The speech was full of homage to Ralph Allen — plus a new Gzowski twist, a kind of Polish-Canadian Don Rickles routine. About one of his best friends, Robert Fulford, Gzowski said "He's the Arnold Edinborough of *The Financial Post*" — i.e. a has-been. I had barely had time to get sick to my stomach when Gzowski wondered aloud "why Zolf would want a senate seat when he has a *sinecure* at the CBC." Calling the guest speaker, whose tributes files contain paeons of praise for his CBC-TV and radio work from well over a hundred CBC colleagues, a do-nothing leech was Gzowski's best Polish joke ever. It was particularly funny coming from Gzowski, the former TV personality, whose audience approval rating for his late-night TV talk show was lower than Morton Downey, Jr.'s.

Gzowski's grace towards me under pressure resulted in my heart pounding, my breath coming with difficulty and a severe anxiety attack seemingly well on its way. Luckily my speech contained many clever put-downs of Gzowski. I was so eager to disgorge them that my fighting spirit returned me to normal.

Worried about health kick-ups, I had arranged to have a

chair to sit in, with an adjacent microphone set up. I realize this was a departure from the Trudeau-Gzowski stand-up gunslinger approach, but that was life. My sitting down in a chair so enraged Fotheringham, he later accused me, in his column, of being a "sit-down comic." I eased into my chair, buried Gzowski in a stream of one-liners that got a rousing response, and then took the high road to my speech. This, my first public speaking effort in years, got a huge round of laughs, which cheered me up and pushed me onwards.

My speech finished, my gut instinct told me to say "good-night" and leave. But I wanted to publicize my book and read from it. I knew I faced surgery soon, but that night I was flying and surely the audience that had lapped up my speech would lap up my literary efforts.

From my seat, with the klieg lights shining in my eyes, making it impossible for me to make out the faces of the audience, I could not get that accurate a read of the audience's response to my story as I read it, briefly, all too briefly. Their response to my story was of course supported by a very drunk gentleman to my left, who I later discovered was the ex-premier of New Brunswick, Richard Hatfield — the biggest political loser ever in the history of the English-speaking world, and an equally drunk cherubic little curmudgeon, who I discovered later was my old colleague, my fellow tipster, my mutual source and my friend — Allan Fotheringham.

Because of the lights I did not know who these baboons were that were preventing my reading of a story at, of all places, a Writers' Development Trust dinner. To the drunk at my left I fought back by suddenly asking, "Can I say something to you in Quaker?" The drunk (Hatfield) said, "Yes!" I then said, "Fuck thee," and got the biggest laugh of the evening.

Buoyed by the laugh, I mistakenly tried to continue to read my story. But the drunks, a minority but a powerful minority of the audience, waved their hankies and shouted for my dismissal.

I decided to throw in the towel. I said, "Fuck it" and brought my papers together, getting ready to leave. Gzowski then decided to play gallant. Gzowski asked for a standing ovation for me. The drunks and boors were already standing and shouting. The rest of the audience stood up and applauded, the drunks continued their shouting, all this mixed emotion giving me one of the weirdest stand-up ovations in the history of Canadian show business.

At the end of the evening many people came over to my table to express their regrets at the boorish outburst of Hatfield, Fotheringham and friends: Robert Fulford; Stevie Cameron; George Anderson (the assistant deputy minister) and Charlotte Gray, writer for *Saturday Night*; John Fraser, editor of *Saturday Night*; Heather Robertson; John Honderich, editor-in-chief of *The Toronto Star*, and his wife, writer Katherine Govier. Katherine told me it was a mistake to read a story before a large audience. Obviously the evening had proved her right. My mistake was my lack of familiarity with Canadian literary conventions; all I had to go by were the huge crowds in Winnipeg I saw come to listen to Yiddish writers read their work. The next day I read Margo Roston's gossip column in the *Ottawa Citizen*. Although she had left early and had not seen the ruckus, Margo brusquely predicted that *Scorpions for Sale* would never be published. (It went on to be nominated for the Stephen Leacock Award.)

I read Fotheringham's column on the Ottawa dinner on my hospital bed in Toronto's Mount Sinai Hospital the night before surgery. Ever the good journalist, ever the good friend and forever in search of any column, at any price, especially the truth, my pal Al trashed me and never once mentioned his own pernicious role in the great Ottawa literary dinner affair. Foth's double standard infuriated me. The beauteous

Susan Teskey, my CBC colleague, came to visit me that night, read the Fotheringham article and dismissed it. "The Ottawa dinner was jammed. All the media heavies," said Teskey. "They know what really happened. Why should anyone believe Fotheringham's version?"

Why, indeed? Foth's role in the literary dinner affair was subsequently trashed by Snider in *Saturday Night,* by Gary Dunford in *The Toronto Sun,* by Martin Knelman in *Toronto Life* and by Heather Robertson in both the *Canadian Forum* and the *Ottawa Citizen* — retribution enough for any nice Jewish boy. (Foth, who prefers dishing it out to being dished, was, I'm told, not amused.) In the process, my book got all the publicity it needed. My most embarrassing moment had in fact turned out to be a mini triumph.

Indeed on CBC-TV's "Midday," ex-Premier Richard Hatfield praised *Scorpions for Sale* as the greatest thing since the invention of the wheel. Foth took me out to lunch and invited me to his home for his book launch. He even paid me the compliment of saying *Scorpions* was too "vicious" to be published.

Still I wonder if Hatfield and Foth hadn't been pissed and pissing on my parade and everybody had listened to my story, who knows, the audience might have all loved it, and then have carried me off the podium in triumph. This way I'll never know. This way the Writers' Development Trust dinner, January 25, 1989, has to remain the most humiliating public experience the Nose That Walks Like A Man has ever endured.

AFTERWORD

Blush, Cringe, Fidget

THE REACTIONS ARE PHYSICAL all right: face turning red and sometimes white, voice switching to falsetto or to bass, stuttering, throat contracting, inhibited breath, dry mouth, stomach contractions, blinking, lowered head and eyes, shaking, fumbling, fidgeting, plucking at the clothes, hands cold and twisting together or held behind the back, smile fixed, feet frozen. These are symptoms of embarrassment, or dis-ease. They are brought on by entirely social and mental conditions, and they constitute proof positive that the human body reacts directly to the mind, even without refeence to will-power or design.

To be embarrassed is to be disclosed, in public. Both factors are important: you must have something to hide first, and you must have an audience. Fall over your shoes as you get out of your solitary bed in the morning, and you may curse but you will not blush: embarrassment is about how you look in *other people's* eyes. (Extremely sensitive people might blush in private — but only when imagining that audience, which remains indispensable to the experience.)

139

The revelation of something we wanted to keep hidden explains the fingering of our clothes: we touch, tighten and arrange, reassuring ourselves that the shell is still in place. Clothes cover what society has decreed shall be concealed; and a good many embarrassing moments involve clothes; lacking them, popping out of them or wearing the wrong ones.

What we would like to hide is most often the truth about ourselves: the inexperience, incompetence and ignorance that lie behind the bombastic or slick facade. To step forward before the expectant crowd with every sign of cool control — and then to fall flat on your face, is to produce embarrassment at nightmare level. The slip on the banana peel, the rug sliding out from under are concrete shorthand for the public fall from grandeur that everyone who is sane can recognize and remember. Failure to live up to expectations is another cause for embarrassment, both for you (provided you understand the extent of your inadequacy) and for everybody watching. The mountain heaves, as Horace put it, and all it brings forth is a mouse.

To *embarrass* originally meant "to hinder by placing a bar or impediment in the way." This creates confusion, as when the march of a column of ants is broken up by a sudden interference — someone "putting their foot in it," perhaps. (In dialects of French and Spanish the equivalents of this word are coarse terms for "to get someone pregnant [*embarazada*]".) Germans use the word *verlegen* — to put something in the wrong place. The original sense of the French *gêne* is "confession." It came to mean the torturing of someone, forcing them to own up; and finally settled down to signify the peculiarly French version of embarrassment.

The specific meaning of *embarrassment* in English arrives fairly late in the language. The term once meant merely "not knowing what to do" in a specific situation, for instance when confronted by a dilemma (as in the French *embarras de choix*), or when there is a superfluity of good things (an *embarras de richesses*). The narrowing of this sense, till we get "an inability to respond where a response is due" approaches the modern English meaning of the word. One can still feel "financially embarrassed," or unable to pay. The sense of inadequacy that having no money can arouse in the breasts of upright citizens was then further honed and differentiated until we get the naming of the precise phenomenon we now call "embarrassment." It still includes occasions where we have to respond but the role we must play is one we have not learned. Examples are finding yourself honoured by a surprise party, or having suddenly to dance in public (if you are not in the habit of dancing, of course).

If, on the other hand, what your image *requires* is a crowd of spectators, then if no one takes any notice of you, that absence will constitute your shame. If you set yourself up to give a speech and no one comes, the lack will hurt as much as being howled down. But even here, embarrassment comes about only if there are *some* people around: the three members who comprise the audience, or the idle ticket sellers who watch you arrive, are needed in order for you to cringe. (Cringing is making yourself small, which is why embarrassment causes the hanging of heads, the shrinking back: these physically express the belittlement you see in the eyes of others.)

There is often complicity in the watching crowd; embarrassment is contagious. So when you step out on stage, or before the TV cameras, and start to sing, only to hear yourself warbling way out of tune, the audience will start to squirm and blush on your behalf. They imagine what it must be like to be you — and they can do it because somewhere in their lives they too have experienced your fate. It is far worse, of course, for members of the crowd who are your friends and relatives, for, as allies, their reputations are vested in your behaving "properly."

The only way socially to pass muster is to "fit in," as we say: to do what is proper, or "fitting." Impropriety, then, is the very stuff of embarrassment. Once again the body comes into play: exposure that is deemed "indecent" evokes embarrassment, and so do flatulence, snores, dribbles, burps and sniffing. You should not be caught talking to yourself either, or picking your nose, or being smelly. To have committed such misdemeanours in public is to die a reputation's death: and it is important to remember that in such cases whether you are to blame or not is of no significance. Your only hope is that the crowd, who usually have an interest in not interrupting the official agenda of the meeting, and in not being contaminated by an impropriety through drawing attention to it, will behave — at least for the moment — as though nothing happened.

Incompetence is what impropriety of the embarrassing kind most often demonstrates. I once said to an important gentleman who arrived to visit my French landlady, *"Madame est sur le téléphone,"* and he answered gravely, *"Cela ne doit pas être très confortable."* The stories travellers bring home from foreign countries often concern the embarrassing results of not knowing what the social norms are: what you should on no account do or say. You bumble ahead with the best intentions, yet commit the offence — and the horror or the amusement you evoke cannot subsequently be put back into the bottle.

Involuntary impropriety is, of course, most acutely embarrassing when you cannot explain away what you have done. What you want more than anything else on earth is an escape from your predicament, and there is none. You are caught and helpless (which is why you wring or hide you hands in reaction to embarrassment). You haven't the vocabulary in the foreign language; or your situation is compromised in such a way that no one would believe your explanation if you gave it, the clues pointing so much more plausibly to what the audience believes they can see. Into this category fall many of the cases of mistaken identity: you hug your husband, whisper extremely private endearments into his ear, then discover to your horror that you have made a mistake: this is not your husband at all. And immediately you know exactly what this total stranger must be thinking: sympathy is essential to embarrassment.

In spite of the great incompetence factor, the embarrassed reaction itself shows not that you lack social adjustment but that you have it, in spades. You *care* what society thinks, and really that is what it wants most. If we look at who most often gets embarrassed, we see that it is sensitive people, people who are trying hard to succeed, who are prepared to mend their ways, who never forget the lesson learned — and what more could society ask? On the whole, people who are never embarrassed (the "shameless") are the most antisocial of us, the least considerate and most uncaring.

The most exquisite kind of embarrassment, and the one that helps us see that the reaction need not merely mean a blind bowing to the pressures of convention, is the horrible realization that you might have hurt someone without intending to do so, or that your own arrogance has made you behave condescendingly where respect was due. Again you have demonstrated incompetence, but here the lesson learned has ethical implications.

Two women discuss, in Norwegian, the handicap of a man with one leg who is sitting opposite them on a subway train. What would it be like to sleep with a one-legged man? The man gets up and says, in faultless Norwegian, "If you would care for a demonstration, Madam, I would be happy to oblige."

A friend of mine, invited by a Kurdish chieftain to a banquet in his mountain cave, decided to wear to the occasion a string of gold beads she had bought in the suq. She was especially proud of her good taste in having spotted and bought them, and decided to wear a little black dress to the feast, to show them off. When she was placed at the party among the women guests, she saw to her astonishment that every woman present was wearing the very same gold beads, but in abundance — massed in necklaces, bangles and fringes, and sewn in profusion all over their clothes. The beads turned out to be traditional signs of dowry and wealth, of the esteem in which a man held his wife. She sat through the meal enduring the pity and concern of everyone present for her meagre lot in life.

My favourite example of this kind of embarrassment happened to John Fraser, the editor of *Saturday Night*. (See the November 1988 *Saturday Night* "Diary.") Visiting one of Jean Vanier's l'Arche communities, he saw a man struggling with a carpentry chore, and spoke to him in a slow clear voice, with the nervously careful solicitude that we all reserve for the mentally retarded. He discovered later that the man was a Sorbonne professor who had taken time off to care for and learn from the handicapped. The way John tells this story, all those listening imagine themselves in the same position, being kind. Then the punch line is delivered, to all of us. Embarrassment, when it is in working order, can produce enlightenment as well as shock.

Precisely because embarrassment often arises from unawareness of important factors in the social environment, and because it is a powerful aid to learning and never forgetting, it most commonly occurs in adolescence. Amost all the good embarrassment stories happened when we were young, and just discovering the mines and traps laid for those who want desperately to find a place among their peers. Very small children know fear and shyness, but they never blush because of social faux pas.

Adults become surer and surer of themselves as well as less and less sensitive, largely through knowing the rules, and through practice and general wear and tear. It often requires decades of experience and self-assurance before the worst of our blunders can be told to other people. Yet even then, what is laughing publicly at ourselves but further social complicity? We have found out not only that everybody else knows what it's like to look a fool, but that a very good way to defuse and rise above a crowd's contempt is to make an even larger crowd laugh *with* you, even if it's at yourself.

CONTRIBUTORS

Ted Allan is a well-known writer of films, novels and stage, radio and television plays. His short stories have appeared in many magazines, including *The New Yorker* and *Harper's*. His original screenplay *Lies My Father Told Me* won him an Academy Award nomination and ACTRA and Etrog awards. Other films are *Love Streams* and *The Making of a Hero*. He co-authored with Sidney Gordon *The Scalpel, the Sword: The Story of Doctor Norman Bethune*.

Charlotte Vale Allen published her first novel in 1976. Since then she has written more than twenty books, including the award-winning *Daddy's Girl*, *Promises* and *The Marmalade Man*. She was born in Toronto in 1941 and currently lives in Connecticut with her daughter.

Margaret Atwood has published more than twenty volumes of poetry, fiction and literary criticism, including the novels *The Edible Woman*, *Surfacing*, *Lady Oracle*, *Life Before Man*, *Bodily Harm*, *The Handmaid's Tale* and *Cat's Eye*. Her work has been translated into more than twenty languages. She lives in Toronto with novelist Graeme Gibson and their daughter Jess.

Jo Anne Williams Bennett won the Seal Books First Novel Award in 1986 for her book *Downfall People* and is currently at work on a second book. She lives in Ottawa with her husband and their three children.

D.M. Clark's first novel, *Inside Shadows*, was published in 1973. He has since written two others, *The Sunshine Man* and *Wild Rose*. Clark and his wife, Luverne, live in Chilliwack, British Columbia.

Matt Cohen was born in Kingston, Ontario in 1942 and educated at the University of Toronto. His first novel was published in 1969. Since then he has received critical acclaim for many books, notably the "Salem novels" — *The Disinherited*, *The Colours of War*, *The Sweet Second Summer of Kitty Malone* and *Flowers of Darkness*. He has contributed articles and short stories to a number of magazines, including *The Malahat Review*, *The Sewanee Review* and *Saturday Night*.

Peter Desbarats became dean of the Graduate School of Journalism at The University of Western Ontario in 1981 after thirty years as a working journalist in print and television. His most recent book is *Guide to Canadian News Media*.

Born in Toronto, but raised in St. Catharines, Ontario, **Howard Engel** was for many years a broadcaster for the CBC in Canada and in Europe. He has written seven mysteries featuring private eye Benny Cooperman: *The Suicide Murders*, *The Ransom Game*, *Murder on Location*, *Murder Sees the Light*, *A City Called July*, *A Victim Must Be Found* and *Dead and Buried*. He is now working on a non-Benny novel set in Paris in 1925.

Helen English is a freelance writer-photographer who has contributed numerous articles to *The Globe and Mail*. She has written one novel about the environment, *House of the Butterfly*, and is at work on a second.

Joy Fielding is the author of eight novels, including *The Deep End*, *The Other Woman*, *Kiss Mommy Goodbye*, *Good Intentions* and, most recently, *Life Penalty*. She is at work on a ninth book. She and her husband, an attorney, live with their two daughters in Toronto.

Born in Hamilton, Ontario, **Sylvia Fraser** worked as a journalist before turning to fiction. Since 1972 she has published five novels: *Pandora*, *The Candy Factory*, *A Casual Affair*, *The Emperor's Virgin* and *Berlin Solstice*. Her most recent book is *My Father's House: A Memoir of Incest and Healing*, for which she received the Canadian Authors Association Non-Fiction Award (1987).

James Houston, an author/artist, lived among the Inuit for twelve years. His involvement in native issues includes terms as chairman of both the Canadian Eskimo Arts Council and the American Indian Arts Center and director of the Association on American Indian Affairs. Houston's books include *The White Dawn*, which was also produced as a film, *Ghost-Fox*, *Spirit Wrestler* and *Eagle Song*. His most recent book, *Running West*, won the Canadian Authors Association Award for Fiction (1990).

Robert Hunter is currently the ecology specialist at CITY TV in Toronto. As an ecological activist, he has written several books: *Warriors of the Rainbow*, *To Save a Whale*, *Greenpeace* and *The Greenpeace Chronicle*. He has also published two books about the intellectual ferment of the sixties: *The Enemies of Anarchy* and *The Storming of the Mind*. His most recent book is *Made in Occupied Canada*.

Martin Knelman is a film and theatre critic and entertainment editor of *Toronto Life*. He has written several books, including *Home Movies: Tales from the Canadian Film World* and *A Stratford Tempest*.

R.D. Lawrence is a Canadian field biologist and the author of sixteen books, including *In Praise of Wolves*, *The Natural History of Canada* and *The White Puma*.

Elliott Leyton teaches in the Department of Anthropology at Memorial University of Newfoundland. He is the author of several books, including *Hunting Humans: The Rise of the Modern Multiple Murderer*.

Roy MacGregor is the author with Ken Dryden of *Home Game*. He has also written *Chief: The Fearless Vision of Billy Diamond* and two novels, *The Last Season* and *Shorelines*. MacGregor works as a columnist for *The Ottawa Citizen*. He lives near Ottawa with his wife, Ellen, and their four children.

Garry Marchant is a Western Canadian writer and journalist who has spent most of his adult life overseas working as a reporter for the *South China Morning Post* and as editor of the *Far Eastern Economic Review* in Hong Kong. He was also an editor of the *Brazil Herald*, the country's only English language daily. His work has appeared in *Away from Home: Canadian Writers in Exotic Places* and *Our American Cousins*, a collection of Canadian writing about the United States.

W.O. Mitchell was born in Weyburn, Saskatchewan in 1914. Educated at the University of Manitoba, he has lived most of his life in Saskatchewan, Ontario and Alberta. As a writer-in-residence at various universities, and a radio personality, he has made his presence felt across the country. His novel *Who Has Seen the Wind* is considered to be the great Canadian classic of growing up. His other books include *Jake and the Kid*, based on his CBC Radio series, *The Vanishing Point*, and *Ladybug, Ladybug . . .*

Farley Mowat has written thirty-two books, many of them about man's relationship to nature. His works include *People of the Deer, Never Cry Wolf, And No Birds Sang, Sea of Slaughter* and *Virunga: The Passion of Dian Fossey*. His most recent book is *Rescue the Earth: Conversations with the Green Crusaders*. Mowat's work has been translated into twenty-three languages and published in more than forty countries.

Alice Munro's latest collection of short stories is *Friend of My Youth*. Her other works include *Lives of Girls and Women, Something I've Been Meaning to Tell You, The Moons of Jupiter, The Progress of Love, Dance of the Happy Shades* and *Who Do You Think You Are?* She has won the Governor General's Award for these last three. Her stories continue to appear in such magazines as *The New Yorker* and *The Atlantic Monthly*. Munro lives in Clinton, Ontario, with her husband.

Journalist **Knowlton Nash** is the anchor of CBC's "Saturday Night" and the Friday and Saturday editions of "The National." From 1978 until 1988, he was chief correspondent and anchor of this program. Nash is the author of numerous books, including *Prime Time at Ten* and *History on the Run: The Trenchcoat Memoirs of a Foreign Correspondent*.

Englishman **Alan Pearson** is a Toronto-based writer and

critic. He has published two books of poetry, the latest of which is *Freewheeling through Gossamer Dragstrips*, and one novella, *In a Bright Land*.

Born in 1931, **Edward O. Phillips** has lived most of his life in Westmount, Montreal, where all his books are set. Phillips's novels include *Sunday's Child, Where There's a Will . . .* , *Hope Springs Eternal* and *Buried on Sunday*, which received an Arthur Ellis Award from the Crime Writers of Canada in 1987. His most recent book is *Sunday Best*.

Garfield Reeves-Stevens has been called "Canada's Stephen King." He has written five novels, the most recent of which is *Dark Matter*. Reeves-Stevens lives in Los Angeles.

Nancy-Gay Rotstein is the author of *China: Shockwaves*, the internationally acclaimed book that was published in Canada, the United States and England. Her previous collections of poetry include *Through the Eyes of a Woman* and *Taking Off*. She received a master's degree in history from the University of Toronto. She holds an LL.B. degree from Osgoode Hall Law School and is a member of the Ontario Bar.

Walter Stewart is a journalist and editor and author of eleven books. His works include *Shrug: Trudeau in Power*, *Towers of Gold — The Canadian Banks* and, most recently, *Wrong End of the Rainbow*, with Eric Kierans.

New Brunswick journalist, humorist, author and historian **Stuart Trueman** was editor of the Saint John *Telegraph-Journal* and the *Evening Times-Globe* for twenty years. He has written three hundred articles for Canadian and U.S. magazines, also fourteen self-illustrated books. Trueman as associate editor writes a weekly feature column for the Saint John newspapers.

Margaret Visser frequently appears on CBC Radio's "Stereo Morning" and "Morningside," popularizing what she calls "the anthropology of everyday life." She is also a regular columnist for *Saturday Night*. Her book *Much Depends on Dinner* was an overnight bestseller and winner of the Glen Fiddich Award, Britain's most prestigious award for books on food.

Born in England, **Eric Wright** came to Canada as a young man. For some years he has lived in Toronto, where in 1983 he wrote his first Inspector Charlie Salter novel, *The Night the Gods Smiled*. The most recent addition to this series is *A Sensitive Case*.

Born in Cheshire, England in 1948, **Tim Wynne-Jones** immigrated to Canada with his family in 1952. Wynne-Jones is the author of seven children's books, as well as several short stories and ten radio plays for the CBC. He has also written the award-winning mystery *Odd's End*, a second novel, *The Knot*, and, most recently, *Fastyngange*.

Larry Zolf is a writer and producer for CBC TV Current Affairs. He can also be heard on CBC Radio's "Sunday Magazine" and CBC TV's "Newsworld." Zolf has written several books, including *Survival of the Fattest: An Irreverent View of the Senate*, *Just Watch Me: Remembering Pierre Trudeau* and, most recently, *Scorpions for Sale*, stories set in the Winnipeg of his childhood, and in Toronto.